THE INTERNATIONAL
PSYCHO-ANALYTICAL
LIBRARY

No. 30

THE WRITINGS OF
ANNA FREUD

Volume I (1922–35)
INTRODUCTION TO PSYCHOANALYSIS
Lectures for Child Analysts and Teachers

Volume II (1936)
THE EGO
AND THE MECHANISMS OF DEFENCE

Volume III (1939–45)
INFANTS WITHOUT FAMILIES
Reports on the Hampstead Nurseries
In collaboration with Dorothy Burlingham

Volume IV (1945–56)
INDICATIONS FOR CHILD ANALYSIS
AND OTHER PAPERS

Volume V (1956–65)
RESEARCH AT THE HAMPSTEAD
CHILD-THERAPY CLINIC AND OTHER PLACES

Volume VI (1965)
NORMALITY AND PATHOLOGY
IN CHILDHOOD
Assessments of Development

Volume VII (1966–70)
PROBLEMS OF PSYCHOANALYTIC
TECHNIQUE AND THERAPY

THE INTERNATIONAL PSYCHO-ANALYTICAL LIBRARY
EDITED BY JOHN D. SUTHERLAND, PH.D., F.R.C.P.E.
No. 30

THE EGO AND THE MECHANISMS OF DEFENCE

ANNA FREUD

Revised edition

LONDON
THE HOGARTH PRESS
AND THE INSTITUTE OF PSYCHO-ANALYSIS
1976

PUBLISHED BY
THE HOGARTH PRESS LTD.
LONDON
*

CLARKE, IRWIN & CO. LTD.
TORONTO

This book was originally published in German
in 1936. The English translation by Cecil
Baines was published in 1937 and reprinted in
1942, 1947, 1954, 1960 and, with a new
Foreword, in 1966. The present revised edition,
based on the 1937 translation, was first published in the United States in 1966, and in this
country in 1968: reprinted in England 1972,
1976.

ISBN 0 7012 0105 3

Printed in Great Britain by
REDWOOD BURN LIMITED
Trowbridge & Esher

Foreword to the 1966 Edition

As indicated in the title, this book deals exclusively with one particular problem, i.e., with the ways and means by which the ego wards off unpleasure and anxiety, and exercises control over impulsive behavior, affects, and instinctive urges.

To investigate an activity of the ego in this painstaking manner, and to treat it on a par with the processes in the unconscious id was a comparatively novel venture at the original date of publication. Much has changed in this respect in the thirty years which have elapsed since then until, by now, the ego as a psychic structure has become a legitimate object of psychoanalytic study. If, in 1936, it was sufficient to enumerate and illustrate ego mechanisms, to inquire into their chronology, and to assess the role of the defense organization as a whole for the maintenance of health or illness, this can no longer be done today without relating the ego's defensive achievements to its other aspects, i.e., to its primary deficiencies, its apparatuses and functions, its autonomies, etc.

It proved not feasible to incorporate such issues into the *Mechanisms of Defense* without carrying out large-scale revisions and without incidentally destroying the unity and present circumscribed usefulness of the book. For this reason it was decided to leave the original text intact, and to relegate more recent thinking to a further volume in which the aspects of *Normality and Pathology in Childhood* are pursued, especially with regard to their developmental and diagnostic implications.

ANNA FREUD, LL.D., Sc.D.

London, February 1966

Contents

Part II

Examples of the Avoidance of Objective Unpleasure and Objective Danger Preliminary Stages of Defense

Part III

Examples of Two Types of Defense

Part IV

Defense Motivated by Fear of the Strength of the Instincts Illustrated by the Phenomena of Puberty

TRANSLATOR'S NOTE

I wish to express my gratitude to Dr. Ernest Jones and Mr. James Strachey for many helpful suggestions.

C.M.B.

Part I

THEORY OF THE MECHANISMS OF DEFENSE

CHAPTER 1

The Ego as the Seat of Observation

DEFINITION OF PSYCHOANALYSIS

There have been periods in the development of psycho-analytic science when the theoretical study of the individual ego was distinctly unpopular. Somehow or other, many analysts had conceived the idea that, in analysis, the value of the scientific and therapeutic work was in direct proportion to the depth of the psychic strata upon which attention was focused. Whenever interest was shifted from the deeper to the more superficial psychic strata—whenever, that is to say, research was deflected from the id to the ego—it was felt that here was a beginning of apostasy from psycho-analysis as a whole. The view held was that the term *psychoanalysis* should be reserved for the new discoveries relating to the unconscious psychic life, i.e., the study of repressed instinctual impulses, affects, and fantasies. With problems such as that of the adjustment of children or adults to the outside world, with concepts of value such as those of health and disease, virtue or vice, psychoanalysis was not properly concerned. It should confine its investigations exclusively to infantile fantasies carried on into adult life, imaginary gratifications, and the punishments apprehended in retribution for these.

Such a definition of psychoanalysis was not infrequently met with in analytic writings and was perhaps warranted by the current usage, which has always treated psychoanalysis and depth psychology as synonymous terms. Moreover, there was some justification for it in the past, for it may be said that from the earliest years of our science its theory, built up as it was on an empirical basis, was pre-eminently a psychology of the unconscious or, as we should say today, of the id. But the definition immediately loses all claim to accuracy when we apply it to psychoanalytic therapy. From the beginning analysis, as a therapeutic method, was concerned with the ego and its aberrations: the investigation of the id and of its mode of operation was always only a means to an end. And the end was invariably the same: the correction of these abnormalities and the restoration of the ego to its integrity.

When the writings of Freud, beginning with *Group Psychology and the Analysis of the Ego* (1921) and *Beyond the Pleasure Principle* (1920), took a fresh direction, the odium of analytic unorthodoxy no longer attached to the study of the ego and interest was definitely focused on the ego institutions. Since then the term "depth psychology" certainly does not cover the whole field of psychoanalytic research. At the present time we should probably define the task of analysis as follows: to acquire the fullest possible knowledge of all the three institutions of which we believe the psychic personality to be constituted and to learn what are their relations to one another and to the outside world. That is to say: in relation to the ego, to explore its contents, its boundaries, and its functions, and to trace the history of its dependence on the outside world, the id, and the superego; and, in relation to the id, to give an account of the instincts, i.e., of the id contents, and to follow them through the transformations which they undergo.

THE ID, THE EGO, AND THE SUPEREGO IN SELF-PERCEPTION

We all know that the three psychic institutions vary greatly in their accessibility to observation. Our knowledge of the id—which was formerly called the system *Ucs.*—can be acquired only through the derivatives which make their way into the systems *Pcs.* and *Cs.* If within the id a state of calm and satisfaction prevails, so that there is no occasion for any instinctual impulse to invade the ego in search of gratification and there to produce feelings of tension and unpleasure, we can learn nothing of the id contents. It follows, at least theoretically, that the id is not under all conditions open to observation.

The situation is, of course, different in the case of the superego. Its contents are for the most part conscious and so can be directly arrived at by endopsychic perception. Nevertheless, our picture of the superego always tends to become hazy when harmonious relations exist between it and the ego. We then say that the two coincide, i.e., at such moments the superego is not perceptible as a separate institution either to the subject himself or to an outside observer. Its outlines become clear only when it confronts the ego with hostility or at least with criticism. The super-ego, like the id, becomes perceptible in the state which it produces within the ego: for instance, when its criticism evokes a sense of guilt.

THE EGO AS OBSERVER

Now this means that the proper field for our observation is always the ego. It is, so to speak, the medium through which we try to get a picture of the other two institutions.

When the relations between the two neighboring powers —ego and id—are peaceful, the former fulfills to admiration its role of observing the latter. Different instinctual impulses are perpetually forcing their way from the id into the ego, where they gain access to the motor apparatus, by means of which they obtain gratification. In favorable cases the ego does not object to the intruder but puts its own energies at the other's disposal and confines itself to perceiving; it notes the onset of the instinctual impulse, the heightening of tension and the feelings of unpleasure by which this is accompanied and, finally, the relief from tension when gratification is experienced. Observation of the whole process gives us a clear and undistorted picture of the instinctual impulse concerned, the quantity of libido with which it is cathected, and the aim which it pursues. The ego, if it assents to the impulse, does not enter into the picture at all.

Unfortunately the passing of instinctual impulses from one institution to the other may be the signal for all manner of conflicts, with the inevitable result that observation of the id is interrupted. On their way to gratification the id impulses must pass through the territory of the ego and here they are in an alien atmosphere. In the id the so-called "primary process" prevails; there is no synthesis of ideas, affects are liable to displacement, opposites are not mutually exclusive and may even coincide, and condensation occurs as a matter of course. The sovereign principle which governs the psychic processes is that of obtaining pleasure. In the ego, on the contrary, the association of ideas is subject to strict conditions, to which we apply the comprehensive term "secondary process"; further, the instinctual impulses can no longer seek direct gratification—they are required to respect the demands of reality and, more than that, to conform to ethical and moral laws by which the superego seeks to control the behavior of the ego. Hence these impulses run the risk of incurring the displeasure of institutions essentially alien to them. They are exposed to criticism and rejection and have to submit to every kind of modification. Peaceful relations between the neighboring powers are at an end. The instinctual impulses continue to pursue their aims with their own peculiar tenacity and energy, and they make hostile incursions into the ego, in the hope of overthrowing it by a surprise attack. The ego on its side becomes suspicious; it proceeds to counterattack and to invade the territory of the id. Its purpose is to put the instincts permanently out of action by means of appropriate defensive measures, designed to secure its own boundaries.

The picture of these processes transmitted to us by means of the ego's faculty of observation is more confused but at the same time much more valuable. It shows us two psychic institutions in action at one and the same moment. No longer do we see an undistorted id impulse but an id impulse modified by some defensive measure on the part of the ego. The task of the analytic observer is to split up the picture, representing as it does a compromise between the separate institutions, into its component parts: the id, the ego, and, it may be, the superego.

INROADS BY THE ID AND BY THE EGO CONSIDERED AS MATERIAL FOR OBSERVATION

In all this we are struck by the fact that the inroads from the one side and from the other are by no means equally valuable from the point of view of observation. All the defensive measures of the ego against the id are carried out silently and invisibly. The most that we can ever do is to reconstruct them in retrospect: we can never really witness them in operation. This statement applies, for instance, to successful repression. The ego knows nothing of it; we are aware of it only subsequently, when it becomes apparent that something is missing. I mean by this that, when we try to form an objective judgment about a particular individual, we realize that certain id impulses are absent which we should expect to make their appearance in the ego in pursuit of gratification. If they never emerge at all, we can only assume that access to the ego is permanently denied to them, i.e., that they have succumbed to repression. But this tells us nothing of the process of repression itself.

The same is true of successful reaction formation, which is one of the most important measures adopted by the ego as a permanent protection against the id. Such formations appear almost unheralded in the ego in the course of a child's development. We cannot always say that the ego's attention had previously been focused on the particular contrary instinctual impulse which the reaction formation replaces. As a rule, the ego knows nothing of the rejection of the impulse or of the whole conflict which has resulted in the implanting of the new characteristic. Analytic observers might easily take it for a spontaneous development of the ego, were it not that definite indications of obsessional exaggeration suggest that it is of the nature of a reaction and that it conceals a long-standing conflict. Here again, observation of the particular mode of defense does not reveal anything of the process by which it has been evolved.

We note that all the important information which we have acquired has been arrived at by the study of inroads from the opposite side, namely, from the id to the ego. The obscurity of a successful repression is only equalled by the transparency of the repressive process when the movement is reversed, i.e., when the repressed material returns, as may be observed in neurosis. Here we can trace every stage in the conflict between the instinctual impulse and the ego's defense. Similarly, reaction formation can best be studied when such formations are in the process of disintegration. In such a case the id's inroad takes the form of a reinforcement of the libidinal cathexis of the primitive instinctual impulse which the reaction formation concealed. This enables the impulse to force its way into consciousness, and, for a time, instinctual impulse and reaction formation are visible within the ego side by side. Owing to another function of the ego—its tendency to synthesis—this condition of affairs, which is particularly favorable for analytic observation, lasts only for a few moments at a time. Then a fresh conflict arises between id derivative and ego activity, a conflict to decide which of the two is to keep the upper

hand or what compromise they will adopt. If through reinforcement of its energic cathexis the defense set up by the
ego is successful, the invading force from the id is routed
and peace reigns once more in the psyche—a situation most
unfruitful for our observations.

CHAPTER 2

The Application of Analytic Technique to the Study of the Psychic Institutions

In my first chapter I have described the conditions under which psychoanalytic observation of the psychic processes has had to be conducted. In what follows I propose to give an account of the way in which our analytic technique, as it has developed, has accommodated itself to these conditions.

HYPNOTIC TECHNIQUE IN THE PREANALYTIC PERIOD

In the hypnotic technique of the preanalytic period the role of the ego was still entirely negative. The purpose of the hypnotist was to arrive at the contents of the unconscious and he regarded the ego merely as a disturbing factor in his work. It was already known that by means of hypnosis it was possible to eliminate, or at any rate to overpower, the patient's ego. The new feature in the technique described in *Studies on Hysteria* (1893-1895) was this: that the physician took advantage of the elimination of the ego to gain access to the patient's unconscious—now known as the id—the way to which had hitherto been blocked by the ego. Thus the goal aimed at was the revelation of the unconscious; the ego was a disturbing factor and hypnosis was a means of getting rid of it temporarily. When a piece of unconscious material came to light in hypnosis, the physician introduced it to the ego, and the effect of thus forcibly bringing it into consciousness was to clear up the symptom. But the ego took no part in the therapeutic process. It tolerated the intruder only so long as it was itself under the influence of the physician who had induced hypnosis. Then it revolted and began a new struggle to defend itself against that element of the id which had been forced upon it, and so the laboriously achieved therapeutic success was vitiated. Thus it came about that the greatest triumph of hypnotic technique—the complete elimination of the ego during the period of investigation—proved prejudicial to permanent results and disillusionment as to the value of the technique set in.

FREE ASSOCIATION

Even in free association—the method which has since replaced hypnosis as an aid to research—the role of the ego is at first still a negative one. It is true that the patient's ego is no longer forcibly eliminated. Instead, it is required to eliminate itself, to refrain from criticizing the associations, and to disregard the claims of logical connection, which are at other times held to be legitimate. The ego is, in fact, requested to be silent and the id is invited to speak and promised that its derivatives shall not encounter the usual difficulties if they emerge into consciousness. Of course, it is never promised that, when they make their appearance in the ego, they will attain their instinctual aim, whatever that may be. The warrant is valid only for their translation into word representations: it does not entitle them to take control of the motor apparatus, which is their real purpose in emerging. Indeed, this apparatus is put out of action in advance by the strict rules of analytic technique. Thus we have to play a double game with the patient's instinctual impulses, on the one hand encouraging them to express themselves and, on the other, steadily refusing them gratification—a procedure which incidentally gives rise to one of the numerous difficulties in the handling of analytic technique.

Even today many beginners in analysis have an idea that it is essential to succeed in inducing their patients really and invariably to give all their associations without modification or inhibition, i.e., to obey implicitly the fundamental rule of analysis. But, even if this ideal were realized, it would not represent an advance, for after all it would simply mean the conjuring up again of the now obsolete situation of hypnosis, with its one-sided concentration on the part of the physician upon the id. Fortunately for analysis such docility in the patient is in practice impossible. The fundamental rule can never be followed beyond a certain point. The ego keeps silence for a time and the id derivatives make use of this pause to force their way into consciousness. The analyst hastens to catch their utterances. Then the ego bestirs itself again, repudiates the attitude of passive tolerance which it has been compelled to assume, and by means of one or other of its customary defense mechanisms intervenes in the flow of associations. The patient transgresses the fundamental rule of analysis, or, as we say, he puts up "resistances." This means that the inroad of the id into the ego has given place to a counterattack by the ego upon the id. The observer's attention is now diverted from the associations to the resistance, i.e., from the content of the id to the activity of the ego. The analyst has an opportunity of witnessing, then and there, the putting into operation by the latter of one of those defensive measures against the id which I have already described and which are so obscure, and it now behoves him to make it the object of his investigation. He then notes that with this change of object the situation in the analysis has suddenly changed. In analyzing the id he is assisted by the spontaneous tendency of the id derivatives to rise to the surface: his exertions and the strivings of the material which he is trying to analyze are similarly directed. In the analysis of the ego's defensive operations there is, of course, no such community of aim. The unconscious elements in the ego have no inclination to become conscious and derive no advantage from so doing. Hence any piece of ego analysis is much less satisfactory than the analysis of the id. It has to proceed by circuitous paths, it cannot follow out the ego activity directly, the only possibility is to reconstruct it from its influence on the patient's associations. From the nature of the effect produced—whether it be omission, reversal, displacement of meaning, etc.—we hope to discover what kind of defense the ego has employed in its intervention. So it is the analyst's business first of all to recognize the defense mechanism. When he has done this, he has accomplished a piece of ego analysis. His next task is to undo what has been done by the defense, i.e., to find out and restore to its place that which has been omitted through repression, to rectify displacements, and to bring that which has been isolated back into its true context. When he has re-established the severed connections, he turns his attention once more from the analysis of the ego to that of the id.

We see then that what concerns us is not simply the enforcement of the fundamental rule of analysis for its own sake but the conflict to which this gives rise. It is only when observation is focused now on the id and now on the ego and the direction of interest is twofold, extending to both sides of the human being whom we have before us, that we can speak of *psychoanalysis*, as distinct from the one-sided method of hypnosis.

The various other means employed in analytic technique can now be classified without difficulty, according to whether the attention of the observer is directed to one side or the other.

INTERPRETATION OF DREAMS

The situation when we are interpreting our patient's dreams and when we are listening to his free associations is the same. The dreamer's psychic state differs little from that of the patient during the analytic hour. When he obeys the fundamental rule of analysis he voluntarily suspends some functions of the ego; in the dreamer this suspension takes place automatically under the influence of sleep. The patient is made to lie at rest on the analyst's couch, in order that he may have no opportunity to gratify his instinctual wishes in action; similarly, in sleep, the motor system is brought to a standstill. And the effect of the censorship, the translation of latent dream thoughts into manifest dream content, with the distortions, condensations, displacements, reversals, and omissions which this involves, corresponds to the distortions which take place in the associations under the pressure of some resistance. Dream interpretation, then, assists us in our investigation of the id, insofar as it is successful in bringing to light latent dream thoughts (id content), and in our investigation of the ego institutions and their defensive operations, insofar as it enables us to reconstruct the measures adopted by the censor from their effect upon the dream thoughts.

INTERPRETATION OF SYMBOLS

One by-product of dream interpretation, namely, the understanding of dream symbols, contributes largely to the success of our study of the id. Symbols are constant and universally valid relations between particular id contents and specific word or thing representations. The knowledge of these relations enables us to draw reliable inferences from conscious manifestations as to the unconscious material behind them, without having first laboriously to reverse some measure which the ego has adopted in defense. The technique of translating symbols is a short cut to understanding, or, more correctly, a way of plunging from the highest strata of consciousness to the lowest strata of the unconscious without pausing at the intermediate strata of former ego activities which may in time past have forced a particular id content to assume a specific ego form. The knowledge of the language of symbols has the same sort of value for the understanding of the id as mathematical formulae have for the solution of typical problems. Such formulae may be used with advantage. It does not matter if one is ignorant of the way in which they were originally arrived at. But, though they help to solve the problems, they do not contribute to our understanding of mathematics. In the same way, by translating symbols we may reveal the contents of the id without really gaining any deeper psychological understanding of the individual with whom we are dealing.

PARAPRAXES

From time to time we obtain further glimpses of the unconscious in another way, in those irruptions of the id which are known as parapraxes. As we know, these irruptions are not confined to the analytic situation. They may occur at any time when, in some special circumstances, the vigilance of the ego is relaxed or diverted and an unconscious impulse (again owing to some special circumstances) is suddenly reinforced. Such parapraxes, especially in the form of slips of the tongue and forgetting, may of course occur in analysis, when they illuminate as with a flash of lightning some part of the unconscious which we have perhaps long been endeavoring to interpret analytically. In the early days of analytic technique such windfalls were welcomed as affording a well-nigh irrefutable proof of the existence of the unconscious to patients who tended to be impervious to analytic insight. Then, too, analysts were glad to be able to demonstrate by means of easily understood examples various mechanisms, such as those of displacement, condensation, and omission. But, generally speaking, the importance of these chance occurrences for analytic technique dwindles in comparison with that of those irruptions of the id which are deliberately brought in to assist our analytic work.

TRANSFERENCE

The same theoretical distinction between observation of the id on the one hand and observation of the ego on the other may be drawn in the case of that which is perhaps the most* powerful instrument in the analyst's hand: the interpretation of the transference. By transference we mean all those impulses experienced by the patient in his relation with the analyst which are not newly created by the objective analytic situation but have their source in early—indeed, the very earliest—object relations and are now merely revived under the influence of the repetition compulsion. Because these impulses are repetitions and not new creations they are of incomparable value as a means of information about the patient's past affective experiences. We shall see that we can distinguish different types of transference phenomena according to the degree of their complexity.

Transference of Libidinal Impulses

The first type of transference is extremely simple. The patient finds himself disturbed in his relation to the analyst by passionate emotions, e.g., love, hate, jealousy, and anxiety, which do not seem to be justified by the facts of the actual situation. The patient himself resists these emotions and feels ashamed, humiliated, and so forth, when they manifest themselves against his will. Often it is only by insisting on the fundamental rule of analysis that we succeed in forcing a passage for them to conscious expression. Further investigation reveals the true character of these affects—they are irruptions of the id. They have their source in old affective constellations, such as the oedipus and the castration complex, and they become comprehensible and indeed are justified if we disengage them from the analytic situation and insert them into some infantile affective situation. When thus put back into their proper place, they help us to fill up an amnestic gap in the patient's past and provide us with fresh information about his infantile instinctual and affective life. Generally he is quite willing to cooperate with us in our interpretation, for he himself feels that the transferred affective impulse is an intrusive foreign body. By putting it back into its place in the past we release him from an impulse in the present which is alien to his ego, thus enabling him to carry on the work of analysis. It should be noted that the interpretation of this first type of transference assists in the observation of the id only.

Transference of Defense

The case alters when we come to the second type of transference. The repetition compulsion, which dominates the patient in the analytic situation, extends not only to former id impulses but equally to former defensive measures against the instincts. Thus he not only transfers undistorted infantile id impulses, which become subject to a censorship on the part of the adult ego secondarily and not until they force their way to conscious expression; he also transfers id impulses in all those forms of distortion which took shape while he was still in infancy. It may happen in extreme cases that the instinctual impulse itself never enters into the transference at all but only the specific defense adopted by the ego against some positive or negative attitude of the libido, as, for instance, the reaction of flight from a positive love fixation in latent female homosexuality or the submissive, feminine-masochistic attitude, to which Wilhelm Reich (1933) has called attention in male patients whose relations to their fathers were once characterized by aggression. In my opinion, we do our patients a great injustice if we describe these transferred defense reactions as "camouflage" or say that the patients are "pulling the analyst's leg" or purposely deceiving him in some other way. And indeed we shall find it hard to induce them by an iron insistence on the fundamental rule, that is to say, by putting pressure upon them to be candid, to expose the id impulse which lies hidden under the defense as manifested in the transference. The patient *is* in fact candid when he gives expression to the impulse or affect in the only way still open to him, namely, in the distorted defensive measure. I think that in such a case the analyst ought not to omit all the intermediate stages in the transformation which the instinct has undergone and endeavor at all costs to arrive directly at the primitive instinctual impulse against which the ego has set up its defense and to introduce it into the patient's consciousness. The more correct method is to change the focus of attention in the analysis, shifting it in the first place from the instinct to the specific mechanism of defense, i.e., from the id to the ego. If we succeed in retracing the path followed by the instinct in its various transformations, the gain in the analysis is twofold. The transference phenomenon which we have interpreted falls into two parts, both of which have their origin in the past: a libidinal or aggressive element, which belongs to the id, and a defense mechanism, which we must attribute to the ego—in the most instructive cases, to the ego of the same infantile period in which the id impulse first arose. Not only do we fill in a gap in the patient's memory of his instinctual life, as we may also do when interpreting the first, simple type of transference, but we acquire information which completes and fills in the gaps in the history of his ego development or, to put it another way, the history of the transformations through which his instincts have passed.

The interpretation of the second type of transference is more fruitful than that of the first type, but it is responsible for most of the technical difficulties which arise between analyst and patient. The latter does not feel the second kind of transference reaction to be a foreign body, and this is not surprising when we reflect how great a part the ego plays— even though it be the ego of earlier years—in its production. It is not easy to convince him of the repetitive nature of these phenomena. The form in which they emerge in his consciousness is ego syntonic. The distortions demanded by the censorship were accomplished long ago and the adult ego sees no reason for being on its guard against their making their appearance in his free associations. By means of rationalization he easily shuts his eyes to the discrepancies between cause and effect which are so noticeable to the observer and make it evident that the transference has no objective justification. When the transference reactions take this form, we cannot count on the patient's willing cooperation, as we can when they are of the type first described. Whenever the interpretation touches on the unknown elements of the ego, its activities in the past, that ego is wholly opposed to the work of analysis. Here evidently we have the situation which we commonly describe by the not very felicitous term "character analysis."

From the theoretical standpoint, the phenomena revealed by interpretation of the transference fall into two groups: that of id contents and that of ego activities, which in each case have been brought into consciousness. The results of interpretation during the patient's free association may be similarly classified: the uninterrupted flow of associations throws light on the contents of the id; the occurrence of a resistance, on the defense mechanisms employed by the ego. The only difference is that interpretations of the transference relate exclusively to the past and may light up in a moment whole periods of the patient's past life, while the id contents revealed in free association are not connected with any particular period and the ego's defensive operations, manifested during the analytic hour in the form of resistance to free association, may belong to his present life also.

Acting in the Transference

Yet another important contribution to our knowledge of the patient is made by a third form of transference. In dream interpretation, free association, the interpretation of resistance, and in the forms of transference hitherto described, the patient as we see him is always inside the analytic situation, i.e., in an unnatural endopsychic state. The relative strength of the two institutions has been altered: the balance is weighted in favor of the id, in the one case through the influence of sleep and, in the other, through the observance of the fundamental rule of analysis. The strength of the ego factors when we encounter them—whether in the form of the dream censorship or in that of resistance to free associations—has always been impaired and their influence diminished, and often it is extremely difficult for us to picture them in their natural magnitude and vigor. We are all familiar with the accusation not infrequently made against analysts—that they may have a good knowledge of a patient's unconscious but are bad judges of his ego. There is probably a certain amount of justification in this criticism, for the analyst lacks opportunities of observing the patient's whole ego in action.

Now an intensification of the transference may occur, during which for the time being the patient ceases to observe the strict rules of analytic treatment and begins to act out in the behavior of his daily life both the instinctual impulses and the defensive reactions which are embodied in his transferred affects. This is what is known as *acting* in the transference—a process in which, strictly speaking, the bounds of analysis have already been overstepped. It is instructive from the analyst's standpoint, in that the patient's psychic structure is thus automatically revealed in its natural proportions. Whenever we succeed in interpreting this "acting," we can divide the transference activities into their component parts and so discover the actual quantity of energy supplied at that particular moment by the different institutions. In contrast to the observations that we made during the patient's free associations, this situation shows us the absolute and the relative amount naturally contributed by each institution.

Although in this respect the interpretation of "acting" in the transference affords us some valuable insight, the therapeutic gain is generally small. The bringing of the unconscious into consciousness and the exercise of therapeutic influence upon the relations between id, ego, and superego clearly depend upon the analytic situation, which is artificially produced and still resembles hypnosis in that the activity of the ego institutions is curtailed. As long as the ego continues to function freely or if it makes common cause with the id and simply carries out its behests, there is but little opportunity for endopsychic displacements and the bringing to bear of influence from without. Hence this third form of transference, which we call *acting*, is even more difficult for the analyst to deal with than the transference of the various modes of defense. It is natural that he should try to restrict it as far as possible by means of the analytic interpretations which he gives and the nonanalytic prohibitions which he imposes.

THE RELATION BETWEEN THE ANALYSIS OF THE ID AND THAT OF THE EGO

I have described in considerable detail how the phenomena of transference come under three headings: transference of libidinal tendencies, transference of defensive attitudes, and acting in the transference. My purpose has been to show that the technical difficulties of analysis are relatively less when it is a question of bringing the id derivatives into consciousness and that they are at their greatest when we have to grapple with the unconscious elements in the ego. This might be better expressed as follows: the difficulty is not inherent in our analytic technique as such; that is no less well adapted to bring into consciousness the unconscious part of the ego than to bring into consciousness the unconscious part of the id or superego. Only, we analysts are less familiar with the difficulties of ego analysis than with those of id analysis. Analytic theory has ceased to hold that the concept of the ego is identical with that of the system of perceptual consciousness; that is to say, we have realized that large portions of the ego institutions are themselves unconscious and require the help of analysis in order to become conscious. The result is that analysis of the ego has assumed a much greater importance in our eyes. Anything which comes into the analysis from the side of the ego is just as good material as an id derivative. We have no right to regard it as simply an interruption to the analysis of the id. But of course anything which comes from the ego is also a resistance in every sense of the word: a force directed against the emerging of the unconscious and so against the work of the analyst. It is our ambition to learn to handle the analysis of a patient's ego, even though it has to be carried through against that ego's will, with at least no less sure a touch than the analysis of his id.

ONE-SIDEDNESS IN ANALYTIC TECHNIQUE AND THE DIFFICULTIES TO WHICH IT LEADS

We know from what has already been said that, if we devote our attention to our patients' free associations and latent dream thoughts, to the translation of symbols and the contents of the transference, whether fantasied or acted, we may make progress in our investigation of the id, but the analysis is one-sided. On the other hand, the study of resistances, of the work of the dream censorship and the various transferred modes of defense against instinctual impulses and fantasies, will assist our investigation of the unknown activities of the ego and the superego, but this method is equally one-sided. If it is true that only a combination of the two lines of research, without a bias in either direction, can produce a complete picture of the analysand's inner situation, then it must also be the case that, if we give the preference to any one of the means of analytic investigation, at the cost of all the others, the result will inevitably be a distorted or at least an incomplete picture of the psychic personality—a travesty of the reality.

For instance, a technique which confined itself too exclusively to translating symbols would be in danger of bringing to light material which consisted, also too exclusively, of id contents. Anyone employing such a technique would naturally be inclined to neglect or at all events to attach less importance to those unconscious elements in the ego institutions which can be brought into consciousness only by some of the other means at our disposal in analysis. One might seek to justify such a technique by saying that there was really no need for it to take the circuitous route by way of the ego, seeing that it could reach the repressed instinctual life directly. Nevertheless, its results would still be incomplete. Only the analysis of the ego's unconscious defensive operations can enable us to reconstruct the transformations which the instincts have undergone. Without a knowledge of these we may, indeed, discover much about the contents of the repressed instinctual wishes and fantasies, but we shall learn little or nothing about the vicissitudes through which they have passed and the various ways in which they enter into the structure of the personality.

A technique which inclined too far in the other direction, so that the foreground was occupied exclusively by the analysis of the patient's resistances, would also be defective in its results, but on the opposite side. This method would give us a picture of the whole structure of the analysand's ego, but depth and completeness in the analysis of his id would have to be sacrificed.

The results of a technique which concentrated too much on the transference would be similar. There is no doubt that patients, when in the state of intensified transference which such a method would foster, produce abundant material from the deepest strata of the id. But, in so doing, they overstep the bounds of the analytic situation. The ego no longer remains outside, its energies diminished, its strength reduced, its attitude that of objective observation, with no active part in what is going on. It is caught up, overwhelmed, swept into action. Even though, under the domination of the repetition compulsion, it behaves wholly as an infantile ego, this does not alter the fact that it is acting instead of analyzing. But this means that such a technique, embarked upon with high hopes of attaining a more profound knowledge of our patients, may end in all those disappointments from the therapeutic standpoint which on theoretical grounds we should naturally expect to result from acting in the transference.

Again, the technique of child analysis which I myself have advocated (1926-1927) is a good example of the dangers of one-sidedness. If we must give up free association, make but a sparing use of the interpretation of symbols, and begin to interpret the transference only at an advanced stage in the treatment, three important avenues to the discovery of id contents and ego activities are closed to us. The question then arises which I propose to answer in the next chapter: how can we make good these deficiencies and, in spite of all, pass beyond the superficial strata of psychic life?

CHAPTER 3

The Ego's Defensive Operations Considered as an Object of Analysis

---

THE RELATION OF THE EGO TO THE ANALYTIC METHOD

The tedious and detailed theoretical discussions contained in the last chapter may for practical purposes be summed up in a few simple sentences. It is the task of the analyst to bring into consciousness that which is unconscious, no matter to which psychic institution it belongs. He directs his attention equally and objectively to the unconscious elements in all three institutions. To put it in another way, when he sets about the work of enlightenment, he takes his stand at a point equidistant from the id, the ego, and the superego.

Unfortunately, however, the clear objectivity of this relation is clouded by various circumstances. The analyst's absence of bias is not reciprocated; the different institutions react to his efforts in different ways. We know that the id impulses have of themselves no inclination to remain unconscious. They naturally tend upward and are perpetually striving to make their way into consciousness and so to achieve gratification or at least to send up derivatives to the surface of consciousness. As I have shown, the analyst's work follows the same direction as, and reinforces, this upward tendency. Thus to the repressed elements in the id he appears in the light of a helper and liberator.

With the ego and the superego the case is different. Insofar as the ego institutions have endeavored to restrain the id impulses by methods of their own, the analyst comes on the scene as a disturber of the peace. In the course of his work he abolishes repressions which have been laboriously achieved and destroys compromise formations whose effect, indeed, was pathological but whose form was perfectly ego syntonic. The analyst's aim in bringing the unconscious into consciousness and the efforts of the ego institutions to master the instinctual life are contrary to one another. Hence, except insofar as the patient's insight into his illness determines matters otherwise, the ego institutions regard the analyst's purpose as a menace.

Following the lines of the exposition given in the last chapter, we shall describe the ego's relation to the work of analysis as threefold. In exercising the faculty of self-observation, of which I have given some account, the ego makes common cause with the analyst; its capacities in this direction are at his service and it transmits to him a picture of the other institutions, drawn from such of their derivatives as make their way into its territory. The ego is antagonistic to the analysis, in that it is unreliable and biased in its self-observation and, while conscientiously registering and passing on certain facts, falsifies and rejects others and prevents them from coming to light—a procedure wholly contrary to the methods of analytic research, which insists on seeing everything that emerges, without discrimination. Finally, the ego is itself the object of analysis, in that the defensive operations in which it is perpetually engaged are carried on unconsciously and can be brought into consciousness only at a considerable expenditure of effort, very much like the unconscious activity of any of the prohibited instinctual impulses.

DEFENSE AGAINST INSTINCT, MANIFESTING ITSELF AS RESISTANCE

In the last chapter I tried for the purposes of this study to draw a theoretical distinction between the analysis of the id and that of the ego, which in our practical work are inseparably bound up with one another. The result of this attempt is simply to corroborate afresh the conclusion to which experience has led us: that in analysis all the material which assists us to analyze the ego makes its appearance in the form of resistance to the analysis of the id. The facts are so self-evident that explanation seems almost superfluous. The ego becomes active in the analysis whenever it desires by means of a counteraction to prevent an inroad by the id. Since it is the aim of the analytic method to enable ideational representatives of repressed instincts to enter consciousness, i.e., to encourage these inroads by the id, the ego's defensive operations against such representatives automatically assume the character of active resistance to analysis. And since, further, the analyst uses his personal influence to secure the observance of the fundamental rule which enables such ideas to emerge in the patient's free associations, the defense set up by the ego against the instincts takes the form of direct opposition to the analyst himself. Hostility to the analyst and a strengthening of the measures designed to prevent the id impulses from emerging coincide automatically. When, at certain moments in the analysis, the defense is withdrawn and instinctual representatives can make their appearance unhindered in the form of free associations, the relation of the ego to the analyst is relieved of disturbance from this quarter.

There are, of course, many possible forms of resistance in analysis besides this particular type. In addition to the so-called ego resistances there are, as we know, the transference resistances, which are differently constituted, and also those opposing forces, so hard to overcome in analysis, which have their source in the repetition compulsion. Thus we cannot say that every resistance is the result of a defensive measure on the part of the ego. But every such defense against the id, if set up during analysis, can be detected only in the form of resistance to the analyst's work. Analysis of ego resistances gives us a good opportunity of observing and bringing into consciousness the ego's unconscious defensive operations in full swing.

DEFENSE AGAINST AFFECTS

We have other opportunities besides those provided by the clashes between ego and instinct for a close observation of the activities of the former. The ego is in conflict not only with those id derivatives which try to make their way into its territory in order to gain access to consciousness and to obtain gratification. It defends itself no less energetically and actively against the affects associated with these instinctual impulses. When repudiating the claims of instinct, its first task must always be to come to terms with these affects. Love, longing, jealousy, mortification, pain, and mourning accompany sexual wishes; hatred, anger, and rage accompany the impulses of aggression; if the instinctual demands with which they are associated are to be warded off, these affects must submit to all the various measures to which the ego resorts in its efforts to master them, i.e., they must undergo a metamorphosis. Whenever transformation of an affect occurs, whether in analysis or outside it, the ego has been at work and we have an opportunity of studying its operations. We know that the fate of the affect associated with an instinctual demand is not simply identical with that of its ideational representative. Obviously, however, one and the same ego can have at its disposal only a limited number of possible means of defense. At particular periods in life and according to its own specific structure, the individual ego selects now one defensive method, now another—it may be repression, displacement, reversal, etc.—and these it can employ both in its conflict with the instincts and in its defense against the liberation of affect. If we know how a particular patient seeks to defend himself against the emergence of his instinctual impulses, i.e., what is the nature of his habitual ego resistances, we can form an idea of his probable attitude toward his own unwelcome affects. If, in another patient, particular forms of affect transformation are strongly in evidence, such as complete suppression of emotion, denial, etc., we shall not be surprised if he adopts the same methods of defense against his instinctual impulses and his free associations. It is the same ego, and in all its conflicts it is more or less consistent in using every means which it has at its command.

PERMANENT DEFENSE PHENOMENA

Another field in which the ego's defensive operations may be studied is that of the phenomena to which Wilhelm Reich (1933) refers in his remarks on "the consistent analysis of resistance." Bodily attitudes such as stiffness and rigidity, personal peculiarities such as a fixed smile, contemptuous, ironical, and arrogant behavior—all these are residues of very vigorous defensive processes in the past, which have become dissociated from their original situations (conflicts with instincts or affects) and have developed into permanent character traits, the "armor-plating of character" (*Charakterpanzerung*, as Reich calls it). When in analysis we succeed in tracing these residues to their historical source, they recover their mobility and cease to block by their fixation our access to the defensive operations upon which the ego is at the moment actively engaged. Since these modes of defense have become permanent, we cannot now bring their emergence and disappearance into relation with the emergence and disappearance of instinctual demands and affects from within or with the occurrence and cessation of situations of temptation and affective stimuli from without. Hence their analysis is a peculiarly laborious process. I am sure that we are justified in placing them in the foreground only when we can detect no trace at all of a present conflict between ego, instinct, and affect. And I am equally sure that there is no justification for restricting the term "analysis of resistance" to the analysis of these particular phenomena, for it should apply to that of all resistances.

SYMPTOM FORMATION

Analysis of the resistances of the ego, of its defensive measures against the instincts, and of the transformations undergone by the affects reveals and brings into consciousness in
a living flow the same methods of defense as meet our eyes
in a state of petrification when we analyze the permanent
"armor-plating of character." We come across them, on a
larger scale and again in a state of fixation, when we study
the formation of neurotic symptoms. For the part played
by the ego in the formation of those compromises which
we call symptoms consists in the unvarying use of a special
method of defense, when confronted with a particular instinctual demand, and the repetition of exactly the same
procedure every time that demand recurs in its stereotyped
form. We know[1] that there is a regular connection between
particular neuroses and special modes of defense, as, for
instance, between hysteria and repression or between obsessional neurosis and the processes of isolation and undoing.
We find the same constant connection between neurosis
and defense mechanism when we study the modes of defense which a patient employs against his affects and the
form of resistance adopted by his ego. The attitude of a
particular individual toward his free associations in analysis
and the manner in which, when left to himself, he masters
the demands of his instincts and wards off unwelcome
affects enable us to deduce *a priori* the nature of his symptom formation. On the other hand, the study of the latter
enables us to infer *a posteriori* what is the structure of his
resistances and of his defense against his affects and in-

---

[1] This point is noted in *Inhibitions, Symptoms, and Anxiety*
(Freud, 1926), see also p. 43, where this passage is quoted.

stincts. We are most familiar with this parallelism in the case of hysteria and obsessional neurosis, where it is especially apparent between the formation of the patient's symptoms and the form assumed by his resistances. The symptom formation of hysterical patients in their conflict with their instincts is based primarily on repression: they exclude from consciousness the ideational representatives of their sexual impulses. The form of their resistance to free association is analogous. Associations which put the ego on its defense are simply dismissed. All that the patient feels is a blank in consciousness. He becomes silent; that is to say, the same interruption occurs in the flow of his associations as took place in his instinctual processes during the formation of his symptoms. On the other hand, we learn that the mode of defense adopted in symptom formation by the ego of the obsessional neurotic is that of isolation. It simply removes the instinctual impulses from their context, while retaining them in consciousness. Accordingly, the resistance of such patients takes a different form. The obsessional patient does not fall silent; he speaks, even when in a state of resistance. But he severs the links between his associations and isolates ideas from affects when he is speaking, so that his associations seem as meaningless on a small scale as his obsessional symptoms on a large scale.

ANALYTIC TECHNIQUE AND THE DEFENSE AGAINST INSTINCTS AND AFFECTS

A young girl came to me to be analyzed on account of states of acute anxiety, which were interfering with her daily life and preventing her regular attendance at school. Although she came because her mother urged her to do so, she showed

no unwillingness to tell me about her life both in the past
and in the present. Her attitude toward me was friendly
and frank, but I noticed that in all her communications she
carefully avoided making any allusion to her symptom. She
never mentioned anxiety attacks which took place between
the analytic sessions. If I myself insisted on bringing her
symptom into the analysis or gave interpretations of her
anxiety which were based on unmistakable indications in
her associations, her friendly attitude changed. On every
such occasion the result was a volley of contemptuous and
mocking remarks. The attempt to find a connection between the patient's attitude and her relation to her mother
was completely unsuccessful. Both in consciousness and in
the unconscious that relation was entirely different. In these
repeated outbursts of contempt and ridicule the analyst
found herself at a loss and the patient was, for the time
being, inaccessible to further analysis. As the analysis went
deeper, however, we found that these affects did not represent a transference reaction in the true sense of the term
and were not connected with the analytic situation at all.
They indicated the patient's customary attitude toward herself whenever emotions of tenderness, longing, or anxiety
were about to emerge in her affective life. The more powerfully the affect forced itself upon her, the more vehemently
and scathingly did she ridicule herself. The analyst became
the recipient of these defensive reactions only secondarily,
because she was encouraging the demands of the patient's
anxiety to be worked over in consciousness. The interpretation of the content of the anxiety, even when this could be
correctly inferred from other communications, could have
no result so long as every approach to the affect only intensified her defensive reaction. It was impossible to make that

content conscious until we had brought into consciousness and so rendered inoperative the patient's method of defending herself against her affects by contemptuous disparagement—a process which had become automatic in every department of her life. Historically this mode of defense by means of ridicule and scorn was explained by her identification of herself with her dead father, who used to try to train the little girl in self-control by making mocking remarks when she gave way to some emotional outburst. The method had become stereotyped through her memory of her father, whom she had loved dearly. The technique necessary in order to understand this case was to begin with the analysis of the patient's defense against her affects and to go on to the elucidation of her resistance in the transference. Then, and then only, was it possible to proceed to the analysis of her anxiety itself and of its antecedents.

From the technical standpoint this parallelism between a patient's defense against his instincts and against his affects, his symptom formation and his resistance, is of great importance, especially in child analysis. The most obvious defect in our technique when analyzing children is the absence of free association. To do without this is very difficult and that not only because it is through the ideational representatives of a patient's instincts, emerging in his free associations, that we learned most about his id. After all, there are other means of obtaining information about the id impulses. The dreams and daydreams of children, the activity of their fantasy in play, their drawings, and so forth reveal their id tendencies in a more undisguised and accessible form than is usual in adults, and in analysis they can almost take the place of the emergence of id derivatives in free association. However, when we dispense with the fundamental rule of analysis, the conflict over its observance also disappears, and it is from that conflict that we derive our knowledge of the ego resistances when we are analyzing adults—our knowledge, that is to say, of the ego's defensive operations against the id derivatives. There is therefore a risk that child analysis may yield a wealth of information about the id but a meager knowledge of the infantile ego.

In the play technique advocated by the English school for the analysis of little children (Melanie Klein, 1932), the lack of free association is made good in the most direct way. These analysts hold that a child's play is equivalent to the associations of adults and they make use of his games for purposes of interpretation in just the same way. The free flow of associations corresponds to the undisturbed progress of the games; interruptions and inhibitions in play are equated with the breaks in free association. It follows that, if we analyze the interruption to play, we discover that it represents a defensive measure on the part of the ego, comparable to resistance in free association.

If for theoretical reasons, as, for instance, because we feel some hesitation in pressing the interpretation of symbols to its extreme limits, we cannot accept this complete equation between free association and play, we must try to substitute some new technical methods in child analysis to assist us in our investigation of the ego. I believe that analysis of the transformations undergone by the child's affects may fill the gap. The affective life of children is less complicated and more transparent than that of adults; we can observe what it is which evokes the affects of the former, whether inside or outside the analytic situation. A child sees more attention paid to another than to himself; now, we say, he will inevitably feel jealousy and mortification. A long-cherished wish is fulfilled: the fulfillment must certainly give him joy. He expects to be punished: he experiences anxiety. Some anticipated and promised pleasure is suddenly deferred or refused: the result is sure to be a sense of disappointment, etc. We expect children normally to react to these particular occurrences with these specific affects. But, contrary to expectation, observation may show us a very different picture. For instance, a child may exhibit indifference when we should have looked for disappointment, exuberant high spirits instead of mortification, excessive tenderness instead of jealousy. In all these cases something has happened to disturb the normal process; the ego has intervened and has caused the affect to be transformed. The analysis and the bringing into consciousness of the specific form of this defense against affect—whether it be reversal, displacement, or complete repression—teach us something of the particular technique adopted by the ego of the child in question and, just like the analysis of resistance, enable us to infer his attitude to his instincts and the nature of his symptom formation. It is therefore a fact of peculiar importance in child analysis that, in observing the affective processes, we are largely independent of the child's voluntary cooperation and his truthfulness or untruthfulness in what he tells us. His affects betray themselves against his will.

The following is an illustration of what I have just said. A certain little boy used to have fits of military enthusiasm whenever there was any occasion for castration anxiety: he would put on a uniform and equip himself with a toy sword and other weapons. After observing him on several such occasions I guessed that he was turning his anxiety into its opposite, namely, into aggressiveness. From that time I had no difficulty in deducing that castration anxiety lay behind all his fits of aggressive behavior. Moreover, I was not surprised to discover that he was an obsessional neurotic, i.e., that there was in his instinctual life a tendency to turn unwelcome impulses into their opposite. One little girl appeared to have no reaction at all to situations of disappointment. All that could be observed was a quivering of one corner of her mouth. She thereby betrayed the capacity of her ego to get rid of unwelcome psychic processes and to replace them by physical ones. In this case we should not be surprised to find that the patient tended to react hysterically in the conflict with her instinctual life. Another girl, still in the latency period, had succeeded in so completely repressing her envy of her little brother's penis—an affect by which her life was entirely dominated—that even in analysis it was exceptionally difficult to detect any traces of it. All that the analyst could observe was that, whenever she had occasion to envy or be jealous of her brother, she began to play a curious imaginary game, in which she herself enacted the part of a magician, who had the power of transforming and otherwise influencing the whole world by his gestures. This child was converting envy into its opposite, into an overinsistence on her own magical powers, by means of which she avoided the painful insight into what she supposed to be her physical inferiority. Her ego made use of the defense mechanism of reversal, a kind of reaction formation against the affect, at the same time betraying its obsessional attitude toward the instinct. Once this was realized, it was easy for the analyst to deduce the presence of penis envy whenever the game of magic recurred. We see, then, that what we acquire by applying this principle is simply a kind of technique for the translation of the defensive utterances of the ego, and this method corresponds almost exactly to the resolution of the ego resistances as they occur in free association. Our purpose is the same as in the analysis of resistance. The more completely we succeed in bringing both the resistance and the defense against affects into consciousness and so rendering them inoperative, the more rapidly shall we advance to an understanding of the id.

CHAPTER 4

The Mechanisms of Defense

PSYCHOANALYTIC THEORY AND THE MECHANISMS OF DEFENSE

The term "defense," which I have used so freely in the three last chapters, is the earliest representative of the dynamic standpoint in psychoanalytic theory. It occurs for the first time in 1894, in Freud's study "The Neuro-Psychoses of Defence," and is employed in this and several of his subsequent works ("The Aetiology of Hysteria," "Further Remarks on the Neuro-Psychoses of Defence") to describe the ego's struggle against painful or unendurable ideas or affects. Later, this term was abandoned and, as time went on, was replaced by that of "repression." The relation between the two concepts, however, remained undetermined. In an appendix to *Inhibitions, Symptoms and Anxiety* (1926) Freud reverted to the old concept of defense, stating that he thought it would undoubtedly be an advantage to use it again, "provided we employ it explicitly as a general designation for all the techniques which the ego makes use of in conflicts which may lead to a neurosis, while we retain the word 'repression' for the special method of defence which the line of approach taken by our investigations made us better acquainted with in the first instance" (p. 163). Here we have direct refutation of the notion that repression occupies a unique position among the psychic processes, and a place is made in psychoanalytic theory for others which serve the same purpose, namely, "the protection of the ego against instinctual demands." The significance of repression is reduced to that of a "special method of defence."

This new conception of the role of repression suggests an inquiry into the other specific modes of defense and a comparison of those so far discovered and described by psychoanalytic investigators.

The same appendix to *Inhibitions, Symptoms and Anxiety* contains the conjecture to which I alluded in the last chapter, namely, that "further investigations may show that there is an intimate connection between special forms of defence and particular illnesses, as, for instance, between repression and hysteria" (p. 164). Regression and reactive alteration of the ego (reaction formation), isolation and "undoing" what has been done are all cited as defensive techniques employed in obsessional neurosis.

A lead having thus been given, it is not difficult to complete the enumeration of the ego's defensive methods as described in Freud's other writings. For instance, in "Jealousy, Paranoia and Homosexuality" (1922), introjection, or identification, and projection are mentioned as important defensive methods employed by the ego in morbid affections of this type and are characterized as "neurotic mechanisms." In his work on the theory of instinct (1915) he describes the processes of turning against the self and reversal, and these he designates as "vicissitudes of instinct." From the point of view of the ego these two latter mechanisms also must come under the heading of methods of defense, for every vicissitude to which the instincts are liable has its origin in some ego activity. Were it not for the intervention of the ego or of those external forces which the ego represents, every instinct would know only one fate —that of gratification. To these nine methods of defense, which are very familiar in the practice and have been exhaustively described in the theoretical writings of psychoanalysis (regression, repression, reaction formation, isolation, undoing, projection, introjection, turning against the self and reversal), we must add a tenth, which pertains rather to the study of the normal than to that of neurosis: sublimation, or displacement of instinctual aims.

So far as we know at present, the ego has these ten different methods at its disposal in its conflicts with instinctual representatives and affects. It is the task of the practicing analyst to discover how far these methods prove effective in the processes of ego resistance and symptom formation which he has the opportunity of observing in individuals.

A COMPARISON OF THE RESULTS ACHIEVED BY THE DIFFERENT MECHANISMS IN INDIVIDUAL CASES

I shall take as an illustration the case of a young woman employed in an institution for children. She was the middle child of several brothers and sisters. Throughout childhood she suffered from passionate penis envy, relating to her elder and her younger brother, and from jealousy, which was repeatedly excited by her mother's successive pregnancies. Finally, envy and jealousy combined in a fierce hostility to her mother. But, since the child's love fixation was no less strong than her hatred, a violent defensive conflict with her negative impulses succeeded an initial period of uninhibited unruliness and naughtiness. She dreaded lest the manifestation of her hate should cause her to lose her mother's love, of which she could not bear to be deprived. She also dreaded that her mother would punish her and she criticized herself most severely for her prohibited longings for revenge. As she entered upon the period of latency, this anxiety situation and conflict of conscience became more and more acute and her ego tried to master her impulses in various ways. In order to solve the problem of ambivalence she displaced outward one side of her ambivalent feeling. Her mother continued to be a love object, but, from that time on, there was always in the girl's life a second important person of the female sex, whom she hated violently. This eased matters: her hatred of the more remote object was not visited with the sense of guilt so mercilessly as was her hatred of her mother. But even the displaced hatred was a source of much suffering. As time went on, it was plain that this first displacement was inadequate as a means of mastering the situation.

The little girl's ego now resorted to a second mechanism. It turned inward the hatred, which hitherto had related exclusively to other people. The child tortured herself with self-accusations and feelings of inferiority and, throughout childhood and adolescence right into adult life, she did everything she could to put herself at a disadvantage and injure her interests, always surrendering her own wishes to the demands made on her by others. To all outward appearance she had become masochistic since adopting this method of defense.

But this measure, too, proved inadequate as a means of mastering the situation. The patient then entered on a process of projection. The hatred which she had felt for female love objects or their substitutes was transformed into the conviction that she herself was hated, slighted or persecuted by them. Her ego thus found relief from the sense of guilt. The naughty child, who cherished wicked feelings against the people around her, underwent a metamorphosis into the victim of cruelty, neglect, and persecution. But the use of this mechanism left upon her character a permanent paranoid imprint, which was a source of very great difficulty to her both in youth and adult years.

The patient was quite grown up when she came to be analyzed. She was not regarded as ill by those who knew her, but her sufferings were acute. In spite of all the energy which her ego had expended upon its defense she had not succeeded in really mastering her anxiety and sense of guilt. On any occasion when her envy, jealousy, and hatred were in danger of activation, she invariably had recourse to all her defense mechanisms. But her emotional conflicts never came to any issue which could set her ego at rest and, apart from this, the final result of all her struggles was meager in the extreme. She succeeded in maintaining the fiction that she loved her mother, but she felt herself to be full of hatred and on this account she despised and mistrusted herself. She did not succeed in preserving the sense of being loved; it had been destroyed by the mechanism of projection. Nor did she succeed in escaping the punishments which she had feared in childhood; by turning her aggressive impulses inward she inflicted upon herself all the suffering which she had formerly anticipated in the form of punishment by her mother. The three mechanisms of which she had made use could not prevent her ego from being in a perpetual state of uneasy tension and vigilance, nor relieve it of the exaggerated demands made upon it and the sense of acute torment from which it suffered.

Let us compare these processes with the corresponding relations in hysteria or obsessional neurosis. We will assume that the problem is the same in each case: how to master that hatred of the mother which springs from penis envy. Hysteria solves it by means of repression. The hatred of the mother is obliterated from consciousness and any possible derivatives which seek entry into the ego are vigorously warded off. The aggressive impulses associated with hatred and the sexual impulses associated with penis envy may be transformed into bodily symptoms, if the patient possesses the capacity for conversion and somatic conditions are favorable. In other cases the ego protects itself against the reactivation of the original conflict by developing a phobia and avoiding the occasions of trouble. It imposes restrictions upon its activity, thus evading any situation which might lead to a return of the repressed impulses.

In obsessional neurosis, as in hysteria, hatred of the mother and penis envy are in the first instance repressed. Subsequently the ego secures itself against their return by means of reaction formations. A child who has been aggressive toward her mother develops an excessive tenderness toward her and is worried about her safety; envy and jealousy are transformed into unselfishness and thoughtfulness for others. By instituting obsessional ceremonials and various precautionary measures she protects the beloved persons from any outbreak of her aggressive impulses, while by means of a moral code of exaggerated strictness she checks the manifestation of her sexual impulses.

A child who masters her infantile conflicts in the hysterical or obsessional manner here described presents a more pathological picture than the patient whose case we first considered. The repression which has taken place has deprived such children of the control of part of their affective life. The original relation to the mother and brothers and the important relation to their own femininity have been withdrawn from further conscious assimilation and have become obsessively and irrevocably fixed in the reactive alteration undergone by the ego. A great part of their activity is consumed in maintaining the anticathexes which are designed subsequently to secure the repression, and this loss of energy is apparent in the inhibition and curtailment of other vital activities. But the ego of the child who has solved her conflicts by means of repression, with all its pathological sequels, is at peace. It suffers secondarily through the consequences of the neurosis which repression has brought upon it. But it has, at least within the limits of the conversion hysteria or obsessional neurosis, bound its anxiety, disposed of its sense of guilt, and gratified its ideas of punishment. The difference is that, if the ego employs repression, the formation of symptoms relieves it of the task of mastering its conflicts, while, if it employs the other defensive methods, it still has to deal with the problem.

In practice, the use of repression as distinct from other defensive methods is less common than a combination in one and the same individual of the two techniques. This

is well illustrated by the history of a patient who also suffered in very early childhood from acute penis envy, in her
case in relation to her father. The sexual fantasies of this
phase reached their climax in the wish to bite off her
father's penis. At this point the ego set up its defense. The
shocking idea was repressed. It was replaced by its opposite
—a general disinclination to bite, which soon developed into
a difficulty in eating, accompanied by hysterical feelings of
disgust. One part of the prohibited impulse—that represented by the oral fantasy—had now been mastered. But
the aggressive content, i.e., the wish to rob her father or a
father substitute, remained in consciousness for a time,
until, as the superego developed, the ego's moral sense repudiated this impulse. By means of a mechanism of displacement, which I shall discuss more fully later, the urge
to rob was transformed into a peculiar kind of contented-
ness and unassumingness. We see that the two successive
methods of defense produced a substratum of hysteria and,
superimposed on this, a specific ego modification, not in
itself of a pathological character.

The impression conveyed by these examples is confirmed
when we examine in detail the effect of the different defense mechanisms in other cases. Theoretically, repression
may be subsumed under the general concept of defense
and placed side by side with the other specific methods.
Nevertheless, from the point of view of efficacy it occupies
a unique position in comparison with the rest. In terms of
quantity it accomplishes more than they; that is to say, it
is capable of mastering powerful instinctual impulses, in
face of which the other defensive measures are quite inef-
fective. It acts once only, though the anticathexis, effected
to secure the repression, is a permanent institution demand-

ing a constant expenditure of energy. The other mechanisms, on the contrary, have to be brought into operation again whenever there is an accession of instinctual energy. But repression is not only the most efficacious, it is also the most dangerous mechanism. The dissociation from the ego entailed by the withdrawal of consciousness from whole tracts of instinctual and affective life may destroy the integrity of the personality for good and all. Thus repression becomes the basis of compromise formation and neurosis. The consequences of the other defensive methods are not less serious but, even when they assume an acute form, they remain more within the limits of the normal. They manifest themselves in innumerable transformations, distortions, and deformities of the ego, which are in part the accompaniment of and in part substitutes for neurosis.

SUGGESTIONS FOR A
CHRONOLOGICAL CLASSIFICATION

Even when we have accorded to repression its exceptional position among the ego's methods of defense, we still feel with regard to the rest that we are including under a single heading a number of heterogeneous phenomena. Methods such as that of isolation and undoing stand side by side with genuine instinctual processes, such as regression, reversal, and turning against the self. Some of these serve to master large quantities of instinct or affect, others only small quantities. The considerations which determine the ego's choice of mechanism remain uncertain. Perhaps repression is preeminently of value in combating sexual wishes, while other methods can more readily be employed against instinctual forces of a different kind, in particular, against aggressive impulses. Or it may be that these other methods have only to complete what repression has left undone or to deal with such prohibited ideas as return to consciousness when repression fails.[1] Or possibly each defense mechanism is first evolved in order to master some specific instinctual urge and so is associated with a particular phase of infantile development.[2]

The appendix to *Inhibitions, Symptoms and Anxiety*, from which I have already quoted more than once, contains a provisional answer to these suggestions. "It may well be that before its sharp cleavage into an ego and an id, and before the formation of a super-ego, the mental apparatus makes use of different methods of defence from those which it employs after it has reached these stages of organization" (p. 164). This may be expanded as follows. Repression consists in the withholding or expulsion of an idea or affect from the conscious ego. It is meaningless to speak of repression where the ego is still merged with the id. Similarly we might suppose that projection and introjection were methods which depended on the differentiation of the ego from the outside world. The expulsion of ideas or affects from the ego and their relegation to the outside world would be a relief to the ego only when it had learned to distinguish itself from that world. Or again, introjection from the outside world into the ego could not be said to have the effect of enriching the latter unless there were already a clear differentiation between that which belonged to the one and that which belonged to the other. But the situation is by no means so simple. In the case of

[1] I am following here a suggestion made by Jeanne Lampl-de Groot during a discussion by the Vienna Society.

[2] According to a suggestion by Helene Deutsch.

projection and introjection the first beginnings are much more obscure.[3] Sublimation, i.e., the displacement of the instinctual aim in conformity with higher social values, presupposes the acceptance or at least the knowledge of such values, that is to say, presupposes the existence of the superego. Accordingly, the defense mechanisms of repression and sublimation could not be employed until relatively late in the process of development, while the position in time which we shall assign to projection and introjection depends upon the theoretical standpoint which happens to be adopted. Such processes as regression, reversal, or turning round upon the self are probably independent of the stage which the psychic structure has reached and as old as the instincts themselves, or at least as old as the conflict between instinctual impulses and any hindrance which they may encounter on their way to gratification. We should not be surprised to find that these are the very earliest defense mechanisms employed by the ego.

But this suggested chronological classification does not accord with our experience that the earliest manifestations of neurosis which we observe in young children are hysterical symptoms, of whose connection with repression there can be no doubt; on the other hand, the genuine masochistic phenomena, which result from the turning round of the instinct upon the self, are very rarely met with in earliest childhood. According to the theory of the English school of analysis, introjection and projection, which in our view should be assigned to the period after the ego has been differentiated from the outside world, are the very processes by which the structure of the ego is developed and

[3] Freud, *Totem and Taboo* (1913, p. 64). Compare also the view held by the English school, to which I refer on pages 52-53.

but for which differentiation would never have taken place. These differences of opinion bring home to us the fact that the chronology of psychic processes is still one of the most obscure fields of analytic theory. We have a good illustration of this in the disputed question of when the individual superego is actually formed. So a classification of the defense mechanisms according to position in time inevitably partakes of all the doubt and uncertainty which even today attach to chronological pronouncements in analysis. It will probably be best to abandon the attempt so to classify them and, instead, to study in detail the situations which call for the defensive reactions.

CHAPTER 5

Orientation of the Processes of Defense According to the Source of Anxiety and Danger

The instinctual dangers against which the ego defends itself are always the same, but its reasons for feeling a particular irruption of instinct to be dangerous may vary.

MOTIVES FOR THE DEFENSE AGAINST INSTINCTS

Superego Anxiety in the Neuroses of Adults

The defensive situation with which we have been longest familiar in analysis and of which our knowledge is most thorough is that which forms the basis of neurosis in adults. The position here is that some instinctual wish seeks to enter consciousness and with the help of the ego to attain gratification. The latter would not be averse to admitting it, but the superego protests. The ego submits to the higher institution and obediently enters into a struggle against the instinctual impulse, with all the consequences which such a struggle entails. The characteristic point about this process is that the ego itself does not regard the impulse which it is fighting as in the least dangerous. The motive which prompts the defense is not originally its own. The instinct is regarded as dangerous because the superego prohibits its gratification and, if it achieves its aim, it will certainly stir up trouble between the ego and the superego. Hence the ego of the adult neurotic fears the instincts because it fears the superego. Its defense is motivated by superego anxiety.

So long as our attention is confined to the defense against instinct set up by adult neurotics we shall regard the superego as a redoubtable force. In this context it appears as the originator of all neuroses. It is the mischief-maker which prevents the ego's coming to a friendly understanding with the instincts. It sets up an ideal standard, according to which sexuality is prohibited and aggression pronounced to be antisocial. It demands a degree of sexual renunciation and restriction of aggression which is incompatible with psychic health. The ego is completely deprived of its independence and reduced to the status of an instrument for the execution of the superego's wishes; the result is that it becomes hostile to instinct and incapable of enjoyment. The study of the situation of defense as revealed in the neurosis of adults impels us to pay very special attention in our therapeutic work to the analysis of the superego. A diminution in its power, a modification of its severity or—as some will go the length of saying—its total abolition

is bound to relieve the ego and to lessen the neurotic conflict, at any rate in one direction. This notion of the superego as the root of all neurotic evil inspires high hopes of a
prophylaxis of the neuroses. If neurosis is produced by the
severity of the superego, then those who bring up children
have only to avoid everything which may contribute to the
formation of a superego of excessive strictness. They must
see to it that their educational methods, which are later
internalized by the superego, are always gentle; the parents'
example, which the superego makes its own by the process
of identification, must be the expression of their real human
weaknesses and their tolerant attitude toward the instincts,
instead of a pretense of an overstrict moral code which it is
quite impossible to put into practice. Again, the child's
aggressiveness must have an outlet in the outside world, so
that it does not become dammed up and turned inward, for,
if it does, it will endow the superego with cruel characteristics. If education succeeds in this, we should suppose that
the human beings thus launched in life would be free from
anxiety, exempt from neurosis, capable of enjoyment, and
no longer torn by inner conflicts. But, in practice, the hope
of extirpating neurosis from human life[1] is found by edu-
cators to be illusory, while from the theoretical point of
view it is shattered as soon as we take our next step in
analytic research.

Objective Anxiety in Infantile Neurosis

The study of defense in infantile neurosis (Freud, 1926,
pp. 108-109) teaches us that the superego is by no means

[1] The most uncompromising exponent of this view is Wilhelm
Reich, but there are many who share his opinion.

an indispensable factor in the formation of the neuroses. Adult neurotics seek to ward off their sexual and aggressive wishes in order not to come into conflict with the superego. Little children treat their instinctual impulses in the same way in order not to transgress their parents' prohibitions. The ego of a little child, like that of an adult, does not combat the instincts of its own accord; its defense is not prompted by its feelings in the matter. It regards the instincts as dangerous because those who bring the child up have forbidden their gratification and an irruption of instinct entails restrictions and the infliction or threat of punishment. Castration anxiety produces in young children the same result as that produced in adult neurotics by anxiety of conscience; the infantile ego fears the instincts because it fears the outside world. Its defense against them is motivated by dread of the outside world, i.e., by objective anxiety.

When we discover that objective anxiety causes the infantile ego to develop the same phobias, obsessional neuroses, hysterical symptoms, and neurotic traits as occur in adults in consequence of their superego anxiety, the power of that institution naturally sinks in our estimation. We realize that what we ascribed to it should really have been put down simply to the anxiety itself. In the formation of neurosis it seems to be a matter of indifference to what that anxiety relates. The crucial point is that, whether it be dread of the outside world or dread of the superego, it is the anxiety which sets the defensive process going. The symptoms which enter consciousness as the ultimate result of this process do not enable us to determine which type of anxiety in the ego has produced them.

If we study this second defense situation—defense against

the instincts from the motive of objective anxiety—we 'shall
form a high estimate of the influence which the outside
world exerts on children and accordingly we shall once
more conceive hopes of an effective prophylaxis of neurosis.
It is pointed out that little children nowadays suffer from
a degree of objective anxiety which is quite unnecessary.
The punishments which they fear may be inflicted upon
them, if they gratify their instincts, are for the most part
altogether obsolete in our present stage of civilization.
Castration is no longer practiced in retribution for prohibited sexual indulgence, nor are acts of aggression punished by mutilation. But, all the same, there is still in our
educational methods a faint resemblance to the barbaric
punishments of earlier times, just enough to arouse some
dim apprehensions and fears, residues handed on by inheritance. Optimists take the point of view that it should
be possible to avoid these remote suggestions of threats of
castration and measures of violence, even now adumbrated,
if not in the disciplinary methods actually employed, at
least in the manner and voice of adults. Those who hold
this view hope that the connection between modern education and these age-old fears of punishment may be finally
severed. Surely, they say, the child's objective anxiety would
then diminish and a radical change would take place in the
relation between his ego and his instincts, which would
mean the final cutting away of much of the ground from
under infantile neurosis.

Instinctual Anxiety (Dread of the Strength of the Instincts)

As before, however, psychoanalytic experience destroys the
prospect of an effective prophylaxis. The human ego by its

very nature is never a promising soil for the unhampered gratification of instinct. I mean by this that the ego is friendly to the instincts only so long as it is itself but little differentiated from the id. When it has evolved from the primary to the secondary process, from the pleasure principle to the reality principle, it has become, as I have already shown, alien territory to the instincts. Its mistrust of their demands is always present but, under normal conditions, hardly noticeable. It is lost sight of in the much more tumultuous warfare waged within its domain by the superego and the outside world against the impulses of the id. However, if the ego feels itself abandoned by these protective higher powers or if the demands of the instinctual impulses become excessive, its mute hostility to instinct is intensified to the point of anxiety. "What it is that the ego fears from the external and from the libidinal danger cannot be specified; we know that the fear is of being overwhelmed or annihilated, but it cannot be grasped analytically" (Freud, 1923, p. 57).[2] Robert Waelder (1930) describes it as the danger that the ego's whole organization may be destroyed or submerged (p. 48). The effect of the anxiety experienced by the ego because of the strength of the instincts is the same as that produced by the superego anxiety or the objective anxiety which so far we have been studying. Defense mechanisms are brought into operation against the instincts, with all the familiar results in the formation of neuroses and neurotic characteristics. In children the

[2] See also *Inhibitions, Symptoms and Anxiety* (1926, p. 94), where we are warned of the danger of overestimating the part played in repression by the superego and stress is laid on the importance of quantitative factors, such as an excessive degree of stimulation.

defense thus prompted can best be studied in cases where great pains have been taken by means of education on analytic lines and by therapeutic analysis to remove those occasions for objective anxiety and anxiety of conscience which otherwise tend to conceal it. In later life we can see it in full force whenever a sudden accession of instinctual energy threatens to upset the balance of the psychic institutions, as is normally the case, owing to physiological changes, at puberty and the climacteric, and occurs for pathological reasons at the beginning of one of the periodic advances which occur in psychosis.

FURTHER MOTIVES FOR THE DEFENSE AGAINST INSTINCT

To these three powerful motives for the defense against instinct (superego anxiety, objective anxiety, anxiety due to the strength of the instincts) must be added those which in later life spring from the ego's need for synthesis. The adult ego requires some sort of harmony between its impulses, and so there arises a series of conflicts of which Alexander (1933) has given a full account. They are conflicts between opposite tendencies, such as homosexuality and heterosexuality, passivity and activity, etc. Which of two opposing impulses is warded off or admitted or what compromise is arrived at between them is again determined in the individual case by the amount of energy with which each is cathected.

The first two of the motives for defense which we have so far studied (superego anxiety and objective anxiety) have, besides, a source in common. If the instinct could achieve gratification in spite of opposition by the superego or the outside world, the result would, indeed, be primarily pleasure but secondarily unpleasure, either as a consequence of the sense of guilt emanating from the unconscious or of the punishments inflicted by the outside world. Hence, when instinctual gratification is warded off from one or the other of these two motives, the defense is undertaken in accordance with the reality principle. Its main purpose is to avoid this secondary pain.

MOTIVES FOR THE DEFENSE AGAINST AFFECTS

Precisely the same reasons as prompt the ego's defense against the instincts underlie its defense against affects. Whenever it seeks to defend itself against instinctual impulses from one of the motives which I have indicated, it is obliged to ward off also the affects associated with the instinctual process. The nature of the affects in question is immaterial: they may be pleasurable, painful or dangerous to the ego. It makes no difference, for the ego is never allowed to experience them exactly as they are. If an affect is associated with a prohibited instinctual process, its fate is decided in advance. The fact that it is so associated suffices to put the ego on guard against it.

So far, the reasons for the defense against affect lie quite simply in the conflict between ego and instinct. There is, however, another and more primitive relation between the ego and the affects which has no counterpart in that of the ego to the instincts. Instinctual gratification is always primarily something pleasurable. But an affect may be primarily pleasurable or painful, according to its nature. If the ego has nothing to object to in a particular instinctual process and so does not ward off an affect on that ground, its attitude toward it will be determined entirely by the pleasure principle: it will welcome pleasurable affects and defend itself against painful ones. Indeed, even if owing to the repression of an instinct the ego is impelled by anxiety and a sense of guilt to defend itself against the accompanying affect, we can still see traces of selection in accordance with the pleasure principle. It is all the more ready to ward off affects associated with prohibited sexual impulses if these affects happen to be distressing, e.g., pain, longing, mourning. On the other hand, it may resist a prohibition somewhat longer in the case of positive affects, simply because they are pleasurable, or may sometimes be persuaded to tolerate them for a short time when they make a sudden irruption into consciousness.

This simple defense against primarily painful affects corresponds to the defense against the primarily painful stimuli which impinge upon the ego from the outside world. We shall see later that the methods employed by children in these primitive forms of defense, which are governed simply by the pleasure principle, are themselves more primitive in character.

VERIFICATION OF OUR CONCLUSIONS
IN ANALYTIC PRACTICE

The facts which have to be laboriously assembled and related in a theoretical exposition can fortunately be brought to light and demonstrated without further difficulty in the analyses of our patients. Whenever by means of analysis we reverse a defensive process, we discover the different factors which have contributed to produce it. We can estimate the amount of energy expended in establishing repressions by the strength of the resistance which we encounter when we seek to lift them. Similarly, we can deduce the motive which prompted a patient's defense against an instinctual impulse from his frame of mind when we reintroduce that impulse into consciousness. If we undo a neurotic defense set up at the instance of the superego, the analysand has a sense of guilt, i.e., he experiences superego anxiety. If, on the other hand, the defense was set up under pressure from the outside world, he experiences objective anxiety. If, when analyzing a child, we revive painful affects which he had warded off, he feels the same intense unpleasure as forced his ego to resort to defensive measures. Finally, if we intervene in a defensive process which was motivated by the patient's dread of the strength of his instincts, precisely that occurs which his ego sought to avoid: the id derivatives, hitherto suppressed, make their way into the territory of the ego and meet with but little opposition.

CONSIDERATIONS BEARING UPON PSYCHOANALYTIC THERAPY

This survey of the defensive processes gives us a very clear idea of the possible points of attack for analytic therapy. In analysis the defensive processes are reversed, a passage back into consciousness is forced for the instinctual impulses or affects which have been warded off, and it is then left to the ego and the superego to come to terms with them on a better basis. The prognosis for the solution of the psychic conflicts is most favorable when the motive for the defense against instinct has been that of superego anxiety. Here the conflict is genuinely endopsychic and a settlement can be arrived at between the different institutions, especially if the superego has become more accessible to reason through the analysis of the identifications upon which it is based and of the aggressiveness which it has made its own. Its dread of the superego having thus been reduced, there is no longer any need for it to resort to defensive methods, with pathological consequences.

But, even when the defense in infantile neurosis has been motivated by objective anxiety, analytic therapy has a good prospect of success. The simplest method—and that least in accordance with the principles of analysis—is for the analyst, when once he has reversed the defensive process in the child's own mind, to try so to influence reality, i.e., those responsible for the child's upbringing, that objective anxiety is reduced, with the result that the ego adopts a less severe attitude toward the instincts and has not to make such great efforts to ward them off. In other cases analysis shows that the various anxieties which have led to the defense belong to an actual situation now long past. The ego recognizes that there is no longer any need to fear it. Or again, what appears to be objective anxiety proves to have its source in exaggerated, crude, and distorted notions of reality, based on primeval situations once actual but now no longer existing. Analysis unmasks this "objective anxiety" and shows that it is a product of fantasy against which it is not worthwhile to assume defensive operations.

When the ego has taken its defensive measures against an affect for the purpose of avoiding unpleasure, something more besides analysis is required to undo them, if the result is to be permanent. The child must learn to tolerate larger and larger quantities of unpleasure without immediately having recourse to his defense mechanisms. It must, however, be admitted that theoretically it is the business of education rather than of analysis to teach him this lesson.

The only pathological states which fail to react favorably to analysis are those based on a defense prompted by the patient's dread of the strength of his instincts. In such a case there is a danger that we may undo the defensive measures of the ego without being able immediately to come to its assistance. In analysis we always reassure the patient who is afraid of admitting his id impulses into consciousness by telling him that, once they are conscious, they are less dangerous and more amenable to control than when unconscious. The only situation in which this promise may prove illusory is that in which the defense has been undertaken because the patient dreads the strength of his instincts. This most deadly struggle of the ego to prevent itself from being submerged by the id, as, for instance, when psychosis is taking one of its periodic turns for the worse, is essentially a matter of quantitative relations. All that the ego asks for in such a conflict is to be reinforced. Insofar as analysis can strengthen it by bringing the unconscious id contents into consciousness, it has a therapeutic effect here also. But, insofar as the bringing of the unconscious activities of the ego into consciousness has the effect of disclosing the defensive processes and rendering them inoperative, the result of analysis is to weaken the ego still further and to advance the pathological process.

Part II

EXAMPLES OF THE AVOIDANCE OF OBJECTIVE UNPLEASURE AND OBJECTIVE DANGER

Preliminary Stages of Defense

CHAPTER 6

Denial in Fantasy

The defensive methods so far discovered by analysis all serve a single purpose—that of assisting the ego in its struggle with its instinctual life. They are motivated by the three principal types of anxiety to which the ego is exposed —instinctual anxiety, objective anxiety, and anxiety of conscience. In addition, the mere struggle of conflicting impulses suffices to set the defense mechanisms in motion.

Psychoanalytic investigation of the problems of defense has developed in the following way: beginning with the conflicts between the id and the ego institutions (as exemplified in hysteria, obsessional neurosis, etc.), it passed on to the struggle between the ego and the superego (in melancholia) and then proceeded to the study of the conflicts between the ego and the outside world (cf. the infantile animal phobia discussed in *Inhibitions, Symptoms and Anxiety*). In all these situations of conflict the person's ego is seeking to repudiate a part of his own id. Thus the institution which sets up the defense and the invading force which is warded off are always the same; the variable factors are the motives which impel the ego to resort to defensive measures. Ultimately all such measures are designed to secure the ego and to save it from experiencing unpleasure.

However, the ego does not defend itself only against the unpleasure arising from within. In the same early period in which it becomes acquainted with dangerous internal instinctual stimuli it also experiences unpleasure which has its source in the outside world. The ego is in close contact with that world, from which it borrows its love objects and derives those impressions which its perception registers and its intelligence assimilates. The greater the importance of the outside world as a source of pleasure and interest, the more opportunity is there to experience unpleasure from that quarter. A little child's ego still lives in accordance with the pleasure principle; it is a long time before it is trained to bear unpleasure. During this period the individual is still too weak to oppose the outside world actively, to defend himself against it by means of physical force or to modify it in accordance with his own will; as a rule the child is too helpless physically to take to flight and his understanding is as yet too limited for him to see the inevitable in the light of reason and submit to it. In this period of immaturity and dependence the ego, besides making efforts to master instinctual stimuli, endeavors in all kinds of ways to defend itself against the objective unpleasure and dangers which menace it.

Since the theory of psychoanalysis is based on the investigation of the neuroses, it is natural that analytic observation should, throughout, have been primarily focused on the inner struggle between the instincts and the ego, of which neurotic symptoms are the sequel. The efforts of the infantile ego to avoid unpleasure by directly resisting external impressions belong to the sphere of normal psychology. Their consequences may be momentous for the formation of the ego and of character, but they are not pathogenic. When this particular ego function is referred to in clinical analytic writings, it is never treated as the main object of investigation but merely as a by-product of observation.

Let us return to the animal phobia of Little Hans. Here we have a clinical example of simultaneous defensive processes directed respectively inward and outward. We are told that the little boy's neurosis was based on impulses quite normally associated with the oedipus complex.[1] He loved his mother and out of jealousy adopted an aggressive attitude toward his father, which secondarily came into conflict with his tender affection for him. These aggressive impulses roused his castration anxiety—which he experienced as objective anxiety—and so the various mechanisms of defense against the instincts were set in motion. The methods employed by his neurosis were *displacement*—from his father to the anxiety animal—and *reversal* of his own threat to his father, that is to say, its transformation into anxiety lest he himself should be threatened by his father. Finally, to complete the distortion of the real picture, there was *regression* to the oral level: the idea of being bitten. The mechanisms employed fulfilled perfectly their purpose of warding off the instinctual impulses; the prohibited libidinal love for his mother and the dangerous aggressiveness toward his father vanished from consciousness. His castration anxiety in relation to his father was bound in the symptom of a fear of horses, but, in accord-

[1] See the description in *Inhibitions, Symptoms and Anxiety* (1926).

ance with the mechanism of phobia, anxiety attacks were avoided by means of a neurotic inhibition—Little Hans gave up going out of doors.

In the analysis of Little Hans these defense mechanisms had to be reversed. His instinctual impulses were freed from distortion and his anxiety was dissociated from the idea of horses and traced back to its real object—his father, after which it was discussed, allayed, and shown to be without objective foundation. His tender attachment to his mother was then free to revive and to be given some expression in conscious behavior, for, now that his castration anxiety had disappeared, his feeling for her was no longer dangerous. Moreover, that anxiety dispelled, there was no need for the regression to which it had driven him and he was able once more to attain to the phallic level of libidinal development. The child's neurosis was cured.

So much for the vicissitudes of the defensive processes which were directed against the instincts.

But, even after analytic interpretation had enabled Little Hans's instinctual life to resume a normal course, his psychic processes were still for a time subject to disturbance. He was constantly confronted with two objective facts with which he could not yet reconcile himself. His own body (in particular his penis) was, of course, smaller than that of his father and so the latter was still marked out as a rival of whom he could not hope to get the better. Thus there remained an objective reason for envy and jealousy. Moreover, these affects extended to his mother and sister: he envied them because, when his mother was attending to the baby's physical needs, the two shared a pleasure, while he himself played the part of a mere onlooker. We could hardly expect a five-year-old child to have enough conscious and reasonable insight to resign himself to these objective frustrations, possibly consoling himself with promises of gratification at some very remote future date or at any rate accepting this unpleasure, as he finally accepted the facts of his infantile instinctual life when once he had consciously recognized them.

From the detailed account of Little Hans's history given in "Analysis of a Phobia in a Five-Year-Old Boy" (1909) we learn that the outcome of these objective frustrations was, in fact, a very different one. At the end of his analysis Hans related two daydreams: the fantasy of having a number of children whom he looked after and cleansed in the water-closet; and, directly afterward, the fantasy of the plumber who took away Hans's buttocks and penis with a pair of pincers, so as to give him larger and finer ones. The analyst (who was Hans's father) had no difficulty in recognizing in these fantasies the fulfillment of the two wishes which had never been fulfilled in reality. Hans now had—at least in imagination—a genital organ like that of his father and also children with whom he could do what his mother did with his little sister.

Even before he produced these fantasies, Little Hans had lost his agoraphobia and now, with this new mental achievement, he at last recovered his good spirits. The fantasies helped him to reconcile himself to reality, just as his neurosis had enabled him to come to terms with his instinctual impulses. We note that conscious insight into the inevitable played no part here. Hans *denied reality by means of his fantasy*; he transformed it to suit his own purposes and to fulfill his own wishes; then, and not till then, could he accept it.

Our study of the defensive processes revealed in the

analysis of Little Hans would suggest that the fate of his neurosis was determined from the moment in which he displaced his aggressiveness and anxiety from his father to horses. But this impression is deceptive. Such a substitution of an animal for a human object is not in itself a neurotic process; it occurs frequently in the normal development of children and, when it does occur, the results vary greatly.

For instance, a seven-year-old boy whom I analyzed used to amuse himself with the following fantasy. He owned a tame lion, which terrified everyone else and loved nobody but him. It came when he called it and followed him like a little dog, wherever he went. He looked after the lion, saw to its food and its comfort in general, and in the evening made a bed for it in his own room. As is usual in daydreams carried on from day to day, the main fantasy became the basis of a number of agreeable episodes. For example, there was a particular daydream in which he went to a fancy-dress ball and told all the people that the lion, which he brought with him, was only a friend in disguise. This was untrue, for the "disguised friend" was really his lion. He delighted in imagining how terrified the people would be if they guessed his secret. At the same time he felt that there was no real reason for their anxiety, for the lion was harmless so long as he kept it under control.

From the little boy's analysis it was easy to see that the lion was a substitute for the father, whom he, like Little Hans, hated and feared as a real rival in relation to his mother. In both children aggressiveness was transformed into anxiety and the affect was displaced from the father onto an animal. But their subsequent methods of dealing with their affects differed. Hans used his fears of horses as the basis of his neurosis, i.e., he imposed upon himself the renunciation of his instinctual desires, internalized the whole conflict, and, in accordance with the mechanism of phobia, avoided situations of temptation. My patient managed things more comfortably for himself. Like Hans in the fantasy about the plumber, he simply denied a painful fact and in his lion fantasy turned it into its pleasurable opposite. He called the anxiety animal his friend, and its strength, instead of being a source of terror, was now at his service. The only indication that in the past the lion had been an anxiety object was the anxiety of the other people, as depicted in the imaginary episodes.[2]

Here is another animal fantasy, produced by a ten-year-old patient. At a certain period in this boy's life, animals played an immensely important part; he would pass hours at a time in daydreams in which they figured, and he even kept written records of some of his imaginary episodes. In this fantasy he owned a huge circus and also was a lion tamer. The most savage wild beasts, which in a state of freedom were deadly enemies, were trained to live together in amity. My little patient tamed them, i.e., he taught them first not to attack one another and then not to attack human beings. When taming them, he never used a whip but went about among them unarmed.

All the episodes in which the animals figured centered in the following story. One day, during a performance in which they were all taking part, a thief who was sitting among the public suddenly fired a pistol at him. Immedi-

---

[2] Berta Bornstein (1936) gives an account of the fantasies of a seven-year-old boy, in which good animals turned into evil ones in a similar way. Every evening the child would put his toy animals round his bed like tutelary deities, but he imagined that in the night they made common cause with a monster which wanted to attack him.

ately the animals banded together to protect him and
dragged the thief out of the crowd, being careful not to
hurt anyone else. The rest of the fantasy was concerned
with the way in which—always out of devotion to their
master—they punished the thief. They kept him a prisoner,
buried him, and triumphantly made an enormous tower
over him out of their own bodies. They then took him to
their den, where he had to stay for three years. Before they
finally released him, a long row of elephants beat him with
their trunks, last of all threatening him with uplifted finger
(!) and warning him never to do it again. This he promised.
"He won't do it any more, as long as I am with my beasts."
After the description of all that the animals inflicted on the
thief there was a curious postscript to this fantasy, contain-
ing the assurance that they fed him very well when he was
their prisoner, so that he did not become weak.

In my seven-year-old patient's fantasy about the lion we
had a bare indication of the working over of the ambivalent
attitude toward the father. The circus fantasy goes con-
siderably further in this respect. By the same process of
reversal the dreaded father of reality is transformed into the
protective beasts of the fantasy, but the dangerous father
object himself reappears in the figure of the thief. In the
story about the lion it was uncertain against whom the
father substitute was really going to protect the child, whose
ownership of the lion merely raised him in a general way
in the estimation of other people. But in the circus fantasy
it is quite clear that the father's strength, embodied in the
wild beasts, served as a protection against the father himself. Once more, the stress laid on the former savageness
of the animals indicates that in the past they were objects

of anxiety. Their strength and adroitness, their trunks and the uplifted finger obviously were really associated with the father. The child attached great importance to these attributes: in his fantasy he took them from the father whom he envied and, having assumed them himself, got the better of him. Thus the roles of the two were reversed. The father was warned "not to do it again" and had to ask for pardon. One remarkable point is that the promise of safety which the animals finally forced him to make to the boy depended on the latter's continued ownership of them. In the "postscript" about the feeding of the thief the other side of the ambivalent relation to the father finally triumphed. Evidently the daydreamer felt obliged to reassure himself that, in spite of all the aggressive acts, there was no need to fear for his father's life.

The themes which appear in the daydreams of these two boys are by no means peculiar to these particular children: they are universal in fairy tales and other children's stories.[3] I recall in this connection the story which we meet with in folklore and fairy tales about the huntsman and the animals. A huntsman was unjustly dismissed by a bad king because of some trivial offense and was evicted from his house in the forest. When the time came for him to go, he took a last walk through the forest, with anger and sadness in his heart. He met successively a lion, a tiger, a panther, a bear, etc. On each occasion he aimed his gun at the big

[3] We are reminded here of the "theme of the helpful animals" which occurs in myths and has been discussed from time to time by psychoanalytic writers, but hitherto from other angles than our present one. See O. Rank, *The Myth of the Birth of the Hero* (1909, p. 88).

beast and each time, to his astonishment, it began to speak and begged him to spare its life:

> "Dear huntsman, let me live
> And I to thee two cubs will give!"[4]

The huntsman always agreed to the bargain and went on his way with the cubs which had been presented to him. He finally assembled an enormous train of young wild animals and, realizing that he now had a formidable host to fight for him, he marched with them to the capital and up to the king's castle. Terrified lest the huntsman should let the animals loose on him, the king redressed the wrong done to him and, moreover, impelled by anxiety, made over to him half of his kingdom and bestowed his daughter on him in marriage.

It is obvious that the huntsman in the fairy tale represents a son in conflict with his father. The struggle between the two is decided in a peculiar, roundabout way. The huntsman refrains from avenging himself on the full-grown wild animal which is the first father substitute. As a recompense he is given the cubs which embody that animal's strength. With his newly acquired force he vanquishes his father and compels him to give him a wife. Once more, the real situation is reversed: a strong son confronts his father who, dismayed at this display of strength, surrenders to him and fulfills all his wishes. The methods employed in the fairy tale are precisely the same as those of my patient's circus fantasy.

Besides the stories about animals, we find in tales for children another counterpart to my little patient's lion fan-

---

[4] "*Lieber Jäger, lass mich leben—Ich will dir auch zwei Junge geben!*"

tasies. In many books for children—perhaps the most striking instances are the stories of *Little Lord Fauntleroy*[5] and
The Little Colonel[6]—there is a small boy or girl who, contrary to all expectations, succeeds in "taming" a bad-
tempered old man, who is powerful or rich and of whom
everybody is afraid. The child alone can touch his heart
and manages to win his love, although he hates everyone
else. Finally, the old man, whom no one else can control
and who cannot control himself, submits to the influence
and control of the little child and is even induced to do
all sorts of good deeds for other people.

These tales, like the animal fantasies, acquire their pleasurable character through the complete reversal of the real
situation. The child appears not only as the person who
owns and controls the powerful father figure (the lion) and
so is superior to everyone around him: he is also the educator, who gradually transforms evil into good. My readers
will remember that the lion in the first fantasy was trained
not to attack human beings and that the circus-master's
animals had to learn first and foremost to control their
aggressive impulses against one another and against mankind. In these tales for children the anxiety relating to the
father has been displaced in the same way as in the animal
fantasies. It betrays itself in the anxiety of other people,
whom the child reassures, but this vicarious anxiety is an
additional source of pleasure.

In Little Hans's two fantasies and the animal fantasies
of my patients the method by which objective unpleasure
and objective anxiety are avoided is very simple. The child's
ego refuses to become aware of some disagreeable reality.

[5] Alice Hodgson Burnett.
[6] Annie Fellows Johnston.

First of all it turns its back on it, denies it, and in imagination reverses the unwelcome facts. Thus the "evil" father becomes in fantasy the protective animal, while the helpless child becomes the master of powerful father substitutes. If the transformation is successful and through the fantasies which the child constructs he becomes insensible of the reality in question, the ego is saved anxiety and has no need to resort to defensive measures against its instinctual impulses and to the formation of neurosis.

This mechanism belongs to a normal phase in the development of the infantile ego, but, if it recurs in later life, it indicates an advanced stage of mental disease. In certain acute psychotic confusional states the patient's ego behaves toward reality in precisely this way. Under the influence of a shock, such as the sudden loss of a love object, it denies the facts and substitutes for the unbearable reality some agreeable delusion.

When we compare children's fantasies with psychotic delusions, we begin to see why the human ego cannot make more extensive use of the mechanism—at once so simple and so supremely efficacious—of denying the existence of objective sources of anxiety and unpleasure. The ego's capacity for denying reality is wholly inconsistent with another function, greatly prized by it—its capacity to recognize and critically to test the reality of objects. In early childhood this inconsistency has as yet no disturbing effect. In Little Hans, the owner of the lion, and the circus-master, the function of reality testing was entirely unimpaired. Of course, they did not really believe in the existence of their animals or in their own superiority to their fathers. Intellectually they were very well able to distinguish between fantasy and fact. But in the sphere of affect they canceled the objective painful facts and performed a hypercathexis of the fantasy in which these were reversed, so that the pleasure which they derived from imagination triumphed over the objective unpleasure.

It is difficult to say when the ego loses the power of surmounting considerable quantities of objective unpleasure by means of fantasy. We know that, even in adult life, daydreams may still play a part, sometimes enlarging the boundaries of a too narrow reality and sometimes completely reversing the real situation. But in adult years a daydream is almost of the nature of a game, a kind of byproduct with but a slight libidinal cathexis; at most it serves to master quite trifling quantities of discomfort or to give the subject an illusory relief from some minor unpleasure. It seems that the original importance of the daydream as a means of defense against objective anxiety is lost when the earliest period of childhood comes to an end. For one thing, we conjecture that the faculty of reality testing is objectively reinforced, so that it can hold its own even in the sphere of affect; we also know that, in later life, the ego's need for synthesis makes it impossible for opposites to coexist; perhaps, too, the attachment of the mature ego to reality is in general stronger than that of the infantile ego, so that, in the nature of the case, fantasy ceases to be so highly prized as in earlier years. At any rate it is certain that in adult life gratification through fantasy is no longer harmless. As soon as more considerable quantities of cathexis are involved, fantasy and reality become incompatible: it must be one or the other. We know, too, that for an id impulse to make an irruption into the ego and there to obtain gratification by means of hallucination spells, for an adult, psychotic disease. An ego which attempts to save itself anxiety and renunciation of instinct and to avoid neurosis by denying reality is overstraining this mechanism. If this happens during the latency period, some abnormal character trait will develop, as was the case with the two boys whose histories I have quoted. If it happens in adult life, the ego's relations to reality will be profoundly shaken.[7]

We do not yet know precisely what takes place in the adult ego when it chooses delusional gratification and renounces the function of reality testing. It severs itself from the outside world and entirely ceases to register external stimuli. In the instinctual life such insensitiveness to inner stimuli can be acquired in only one way—by the mechanism of repression.

---

[7] I would remind my readers that the relation of the mechanism of denial to psychic disease and to character formation has recently been discussed by several writers. Helene Deutsch (1933) deals with the significance of this defensive process in the genesis of chronic hypomania. Bertram D. Lewin (1932) describes how this same mechanism is employed by the newly formed pleasure ego of the hypomanic patient. Anny Angel (1934) points out the connection between denial and optimism.

CHAPTER 7

Denial in Word and Act

For some years the infantile ego is free to get rid of unwelcome facts by denying them, while retaining its faculty of reality testing unimpaired. It makes the fullest possible use of this power, not confining itself exclusively to the sphere of ideas and fantasy, for it does not merely think, it acts. It utilizes all manner of external objects in dramatizing its reversal of real situations. The denial of reality also is, of course, one of the many motives underlying children's play in general and games of impersonation in particular.

I am reminded here of a little book of verses by an English writer, in which the juxtaposition of fantasy and fact in the life of its child hero is described in a particularly delightful way. I refer to *When We Were Very Young*, by A. A. Milne. In the nursery of this three-year-old there are four chairs. When he sits on the first, he *is* an explorer, sailing up the Amazon by night. On the second he is a lion, frightening his nurse with a roar; on the third he is a captain, steering his ship over the sea. But on the fourth, a

child's high chair, he *tries to pretend* that he is simply himself, just a little boy. It is not difficult to see the author's
meaning: the elements for the construction of a pleasurable
world of fantasy lie ready to the child's hand, but his task
and his achievement are to recognize and assimilate the
facts of reality.

It is a curious thing that adults are so ready to make use
of this very mechanism in their intercourse with children.
Much of the pleasure which they give to children is derived.
from this kind of denial of reality. It is quite a common
thing to tell even a small child "what a big boy" he is and
to declare, contrary to the obvious facts, that he is as strong
"as Father," as clever "as Mother," as brave "as a soldier"
or as "tough" as his "big brother." It is more natural that,
when people want to comfort a child, they resort to these
reversals of the real facts. The grown-ups assure him, when
he has hurt himself, that he is "better now" or that some
food which he loathes "isn't a bit nasty" or, when he is
distressed because somebody has gone away, we tell him
that he or she will be "back soon." Some children actually
pick up these consolatory formulae and employ a stereotyped phrase to describe what is painful. For instance, one
little girl of two years used, whenever her mother left the
room, to announce the fact by a mechanical murmur of
"Mummy coming soon." Another (English) child used to
call out in a lamentable voice, whenever he had to take
nasty medicine, "like it, like it"—a fragment of a sentence
used by his nurse to encourage him to think that the drops
tasted good.

Many of the presents brought to children by grown-up
visitors minister to the same illusion. A small handbag or
a tiny sunshade or umbrella is intended to help a little girl

to pretend to be a "grown-up lady"; a walking stick, a uniform, and toy weapons of different sorts enable a little boy to ape manhood. Indeed, even dolls, besides being useful for all sorts of other games, create the fiction of motherhood, while railways, motors, and bricks not only serve to fulfill various wishes and provide opportunities for sublimation but produce in the minds of children the agreeable fantasy that they can control the world. At this point we pass from the study of the processes of defense and avoidance, properly so-called, to that of the conditions of children's play, a subject which is being exhaustively discussed from different angles by academic psychology.

All this suggests another reason in theory for the perennial conflict between the different methods of educating children (Froebel versus Montessori). The real point at issue is how far it must be the task of education to induce children of even the tenderest years to devote all their efforts to assimilating reality and how far it is permissible to encourage them to turn away from reality and construct a world of fantasy.

When grown-up people consent to enter into the fictions whereby children transform a painful reality into its opposite, they invariably do so under certain strict conditions. Children are expected to keep the enacting of their fantasies within well-defined limits. A child who has just been a horse or an elephant, going about on all fours, neighing or trumpeting, must be prepared at a moment's notice to take his place at table and be quiet and well-behaved. The lion tamer must himself be ready to obey his nursemaid, and the explorer or pirate must submit to be sent to bed just when the most interesting things are beginning to happen in the world of grown-ups. The indulgent attitude of the latter toward the child's mechanism of denial vanishes the moment that he ceases to make the transition from fantasy to reality readily, without any delay or hitch, or tries to shape his actual behavior according to his fantasies—to put it more exactly, the moment his fantasy activity ceases to be a game and becomes an automatism or an obsession.

One little girl whom I had the opportunity of observing could not make up her mind to the fact of the difference between the sexes. She had one older and one younger brother and the comparison of herself with them was a constant source of acute unpleasure, which impelled her somehow to defend herself against it or to "work it over." At the same time exhibitionism played a considerable part in the development of her instinctual life, and so her envy and her wish for a penis took the form of a desire to have, like her brothers, something to display. We know from what happens in the case of other children that there are various ways in which she might have fulfilled this wish. For instance, the craving to exhibit something might have been displaced from the genitals to the rest of her pretty body. Or she might have developed an interest in beautiful clothes and have become "vain." Or again, she might have set herself to excel in drill and gymnastics, as a substitute for the acrobatics of her brothers' genitals. The way she actually chose was a shorter one. She denied the fact that she had not got a penis and so saved herself the trouble of finding a substitute and, from that time on, she suffered from a kind of compulsion to display the nonexistent organ. In the physical sphere this compulsion took the form of occasionally lifting up her skirts and exhibiting herself. The meaning of this was, "Look what a fine thing I've got!" In her daily life she would call to the others on every conceivable occasion to come and admire something which was not there at all.[1] "Come and see what a lot of eggs the hens have laid!" "Listen, there's the car with uncle!" Actually, no eggs had been laid, nor was there any sign of the car for which they were eagerly watching. At first, her elders greeted these jokes with laughter and applause, but the sudden and repeated disappointments thus inflicted on them reduced her brothers and sisters to floods of tears. Her behavior at this time might be said to be on the borderline between play and obsession.

We see the same process even more plainly in the seven-year-old lion tamer of the last chapter. As his analysis showed, his fantasies represented not merely a compensation for residues of unpleasure and uneasiness but an attempt to master the whole of his acute castration anxiety. The habit of denial grew upon him, till he could no longer keep pace with his craving to transform anxiety objects into friendly beings who would either protect or obey him. He redoubled his efforts; the tendency to belittle all that terrified him increased. Whatever roused his anxiety became an object of ridicule and, since everything around him was a source of anxiety, the whole world took on an aspect of absurdity. His reaction to the constant pressure of castration anxiety was a no less constant facetiousness. At first, this struck one as merely playful, but its obsessional character was betrayed by the fact that he was never free from anxiety except when joking and that, if he tried to approach the outside world in a more serious spirit, he paid for it with anxiety attacks.

[1] Compare S. Rádo's (1933) notion of the "wish-penis" of little girls, which he describes as the hallucinatory reproduction of the male organ which they have seen.

We do not as a rule see anything abnormal in the small boy who wants to be a big man and plays at being "Daddy," having borrowed his father's hat and stick for the purpose. At any rate he is a very familiar figure. I was told that this used to be a favorite game of one of my child patients, who, when I knew him, would fall into a state of extreme ill humor whenever he saw an unusually tall or powerful man. He used to put on his father's hat and walk about in it. As long as nobody interfered with him, he was contented and happy. In the same way, during the whole of one summer holiday he went about with a full rucksack on his back. The difference between him and the little boy who plays at being a big man is simply that my small patient's play was earnest, for, whenever he was forced to take off the hat indoors, at meals or when he went to bed, he reacted with restlessness and ill humor.

On being given a peaked cap which had a "grown-up" appearance, the little boy repeated the behavior originally associated with his father's hat. He carried the cap everywhere with him, clutching it convulsively in his hand, if he was not allowed to wear it. Of course, he constantly found that he wanted to use his hands for other purposes. On one such occasion, when he was anxiously looking around for somewhere to put his cap, the possibilities of the flap in front of his leather breeches dawned upon him. Without more ado he thrust the cap into the opening and so had his hands free and concluded to his great relief that now he need never be parted from his treasure. Clearly it had arrived at the place where, according to its symbolic significance, it had always belonged: it was in immediate proximity to his genitals.

In the foregoing account I have several times, for want of

a better word, described the behavior of these children as obsessional. To the superficial observer it has indeed a very great resemblance to the symptoms of obsessional neurosis. If, however, we examine the children's actions more closely, we see that they are not obsessional in the strict sense of the term. Their structure is entirely different from that which we know to be characteristic of neurotic symptoms in general. It is true that, as in the formation of the latter, the process leading up to them begins with some objective frustration or disappointment, but the ensuing conflict is not thereupon internalized: it preserves its connection with the outside world. The defensive measure to which the ego has recourse is aimed not against the instinctual life but directly at the external world which inflicts the frustration. Just as, in the neurotic conflict, perception of a prohibited instinctual stimulus is warded off by means of repression, so the infantile ego resorts to denial in order not to become aware of some painful impression from without. In obsessional neurosis the repression is secured by means of a reaction formation, which contains the reverse of the repressed instinctual impulse (sympathy instead of cruelty, bashfulness instead of exhibitionism). Similarly, in the infantile situations which I have described, the denial of reality is completed and confirmed when in his fantasies, words or behavior, the child reverses the real facts. The maintenance of obsessional reaction formations demands the constant expenditure of energy which we call anticathexis. A similar expenditure is necessary in order that the child's ego may maintain and dramatize his pleasurable fantasies. The masculinity of the brothers of the little girl whose case I have quoted was constantly paraded before her eyes: with equal regularity she responded with the assurance, "I have got something to show too." The envy of the little boy with the cap was continually excited by the men whom he saw around him, so he confronted them persistently with the hat, cap or rucksack which he regarded as a tangible proof of his own masculinity. Any external interference with this kind of behavior produces the same result as when genuinely obsessional activities are thus obstructed. The balance, laboriously preserved, between the tendency which is warded off and the defending force is upset, the external stimulus which has been denied or the instinctual stimulus which has been repressed seeks to force its way into consciousness and produces in the ego feelings of anxiety and unpleasure.

The defensive method of denial by word and act is subject to the same restrictions in time as I have discussed in the previous chapter in connection with denial in fantasy.[2] It can be employed only so long as it can exist side by side with the capacity for reality testing without disturbing it. The organization of the mature ego becomes unified through synthesis and this method of denial is then discarded and is resumed only if the relation to reality has been gravely disturbed and the function of reality testing suspended. In psychotic delusions, for instance, a piece of wood may represent love objects which the patient longs for or has lost, just as children use similar things to protect them.[3] The single possible exception in neurosis is the "talisman" of obsessional neurotics, but I should not care to commit myself to an opinion as to whether the possession to which such patients cling so strenuously represents

[2] "Impersonation" in children's play, which I shall not attempt to analyze in detail here, comes halfway between "denial in word and act" and "denial in fantasy."

[3] Compare R. Laforgue's notion of scotomization (1928).

a protection against prohibited impulses from within or against dangerous forces from without, or whether perhaps it combines both types of defense.

The method of denial in word and act is subject to a second restriction, which does not apply to denial in fantasy. In his fantasies a child is supreme. So long as he does not tell them to anybody, no one has any reason to interfere. On the other hand, dramatization of fantasies in word and act requires a stage in the outside world. So his employment of this mechanism is conditioned externally by the extent to which those around him will fall in with his dramatization, just as it is conditioned internally by the degree of compatibility with the function of reality testing. In the case of the boy with the cap, for instance, the success of his efforts at defense depended entirely on his being allowed to wear it in the house, at school, and in the kindergarten. People in general, on the other hand, judge the normality or abnormality of such protective mechanisms not by the inner structure of the defensive measure but by the degree of its conspicuousness. So long as the little boy's obsession took the form of going about with the hat, he had a "symptom." He was regarded as an odd child and was always in danger of being bereft of the thing which protected him from anxiety. At a later period in his life, his desire for protection became less noticeable. He laid aside his rucksack and headgear and contented himself with carrying a pencil in his pocket. From that time he was regarded as normal. He had adapted his mechanism to suit his environment, or at least he concealed it and did not allow it to conflict with other people's requirements. But this did not mean that there was any change in the inner anxiety situation. For the denial of his castration anxiety he was dependent in no less obsessional a fashion on carrying about his pencil and, if he happened to lose it or not to have it with him, he suffered from attacks of anxiety and unpleasure, just as he had formerly suffered.

The fate of anxiety is sometimes determined by the indulgence extended by other people to such protective measures. It may be that the anxiety will stop at that point and remain bound in the original "symptom" or, if the attempt at defense fails, there may be a further development, leading directly to internal conflict, to the turning of the defensive struggle against the instinctual life and so to genuine neurotic elaboration. But it would be dangerous to try to guard against infantile neuroses by falling in with the child's denial of reality. When employed to excess, it is a mechanism which produces in the ego excrescences, eccentricities, and idiosyncrasies, of which, once the period of primitive denial is finally past, it is hard to get rid.

CHAPTER 8

Restriction of the Ego

Our comparison of the mechanisms of denial and repression, fantasy formation and reaction formation has revealed a parallelism in the methods adopted by the ego for the avoidance of unpleasure from external and from internal sources. We trace the same parallelism when we study another, simpler defense mechanism. The method of denial, upon which is based the fantasy of the reversal of the real facts into their opposite, is employed in situations in which it is impossible to escape some painful external impression. When a child is somewhat older, his greater freedom of physical movement and his increased powers of psychic activity enable his ego to evade such stimuli and there is no need for him to perform so complicated a psychic operation as that of denial. Instead of perceiving the painful impression and subsequently canceling it by withdrawing its cathexis, it is open to the ego to refuse to encounter the dangerous external situation at all. It can take to flight and so, in the truest sense of the word, "avoid" the occasions of unpleasure. The mechanism of avoidance is so primitive and natural and, moreover, so inseparably associated with the normal development of the ego that it is not easy, for purposes of theoretical discussion, to detach it from its usual context and to view it in isolation.

When I was analyzing the little boy whom I introduced in the previous chapter as "the boy with the cap," I was able to observe how his avoidance of unpleasure developed on these lines. One day, when he was at my house, he found a little magic drawing block, which appealed to him greatly. He began enthusiastically to rub the pages, one by one, with a colored pencil and was pleased when I did the same. Suddenly, however, he glanced at what I was doing, came to a stop, and was evidently upset. The next moment he put down his pencil, pushed the whole apparatus (hitherto jealously guarded) across to me, stood up, and said, "You go on doing it; I would much rather watch." Obviously, when he looked at my drawing, it struck him as more beautiful, more skillful, or somehow more perfect than his own, and the comparison gave him a shock. He instantly decided that he would not compete with me any more, since the results were disagreeable, and thereupon he abandoned the activity which, a moment ago, had given him pleasure. He adopted the role of the spectator, who does nothing and so cannot have his performance compared with that of someone else. By imposing this restriction on himself the child avoided a repetition of the disagreeable impression.

This incident was not an isolated one. A game with me in which he did not win, a transfer picture which was not as good as one of mine—in fact, anything which he could not do quite as well as I could was enough to produce the same sudden change of mood. He lost all pleasure in what he was doing, gave it up, and automatically, as it seemed, ceased to be interested in it. On the other hand, he would become obsessed with occupations in which he felt himself to be my superior and would spend unlimited time on them. It was only natural that, when he first went to school, he behaved just as he did with me. He steadily refused to join the other children in any game or lesson in which he did not feel quite sure of himself. He would go from one child to another and "look on." His method of mastering unpleasure by reversing it into something pleasurable had undergone a change. He restricted the functioning of his ego and drew back, greatly to the detriment of his development, from any external situation which might possibly give rise to the type of unpleasure which he feared most. Only when he was with children much younger than himself did he get rid of these restrictions and take an active interest in their doings.

In kindergartens and schools run on modern lines, where less prominence is given to class teaching than to self-chosen, individual work, children of the type of my little boy with the cap are not at all rare. Teachers tell us that a new intermediate class of children has sprung up between the familiar groups of those who are intelligent, interested, and diligent, on the one hand and, on the other, those who are intellectually duller and whom it is hard to interest and to induce to work, and that this new type cannot at first sight be placed in any of the usual categories of pupils with inhibitions in learning. Although these children are distinctly intelligent and quite well developed and although they are popular with their school fellows, they cannot be induced to take their place in the regular games or lessons. In spite of the fact that the method used in the school is scrupulously to avoid criticism and blame, they behave as if they were intimidated. The mere comparison of their achievements with those of the other children robs their work of all its value in their eyes. If they fail in a task or a constructive game, they conceive a permanent disinclination to repeat the attempt. So they remain inactive and reluctant to bind themselves to any place or occupation, contenting themselves with looking on at the work of the others. Secondarily, their idling about has an antisocial effect, for, being bored, they begin to quarrel with the children who are absorbed in work or play.

The contrast between the good abilities and the disappointing performance of these children suggests that they are neurotically inhibited and that the disturbance from which they suffer is based on processes and contents familiar to us from the analysis of genuine inhibitions. The picture in both cases shows the same relation to the past. In neither is the symptom related to its real object but to a substitute in the present for some dominant interest in the past. For instance, when a child is inhibited in reckoning or thinking, an adult in speaking or a musician in playing, the real activity avoided is not that of dealing mentally with ideas or numbers, pronouncing words, drawing the bow across the strings or touching the keys of the piano. Such activities on the part of the ego are in themselves harmless, but they have become related to past sexual activities, which the subject has warded off; these they now represent and, having thus become "sexualized," they are themselves the object of the ego's defensive operations. Similarly, when children defend themselves against the unpleasure which they experience on comparing their own performances with those of others, the feeling in question is merely substitutive. The sight of another person's superior achievement signifies (or at least it did so in my patient) the sight of genitals larger than their own, and these they envy. Again, when they are encouraged to emulate their fellows, it suggests the hopeless rivalry of the oedipus phase or the disagreeable realization of the difference between the sexes.

In one respect, however, the two kinds of disturbance differ. The children who insist on playing the part of spectators recover their capacity for work if the conditions under which they have to work are changed. Genuine inhibitions, on the other hand, do not vary and changes in the environment hardly affect them. One little girl of the former type was obliged for external reasons to stay away for a time from her first school, where it had been her habit to "look on." She was taught privately and she at once mastered, in the form of play, lessons which had remained a closed book to her so long as she was with other children. I know of a similar instance of a complete turnabout in another little girl of seven. As she was backward at school, she had some private coaching. In these lessons at home her behavior was normal and there was no sign of any inhibition, but she was quite unable to produce these good results at school, where the lessons were on just the same lines. Thus, these two little girls could learn, provided that there was no question of their achievements being compared with those of other children, just as the little boy whom I analyzed could take part in the games of younger but not of older playmates. To outward appearance such children behave as if the activities in question were subject to both an inner and an external prohibition. In reality, however, the check is automatic and takes place as soon as a particular activity results in a disagreeable impression. The psychic situation of these children is similar to that which the study of femininity has shown to be characteristic of little girls at a particular turning point in their development.[1] Independently of any fear of punishment or anxiety of conscience, a little girl at a certain period in her life gives up clitoral masturbation, thus restricting her masculine strivings. Her self-love is mortified when she compares herself with boys, who are better equipped for masturbation, and she does not want to be constantly reminded of her disadvantages by indulging in the practice.

It would be a mistake to suppose that such restrictions are imposed on the ego only for the purpose of avoiding the unpleasure ensuing from a realization of inferiority to others, i.e., from disappointment and discouragement. In the analysis of a ten-year-old boy I observed such restriction of activity take place, as a transitory symptom, for the purpose of avoiding immediate objective anxiety. But this child had the opposite reason for his anxiety. During a certain phase in his analysis he developed into a brilliant football player. His prowess was recognized by the big boys at his school and to his great delight they let him join in their games, although he was much younger than they. Before long, he reported the following dream. He was playing football and a big boy kicked the ball with such force that my patient had to jump over it in order not to be hit. He awoke with feelings of anxiety. The interpretation of the dream showed that his pride in associating with the big boys had soon turned into anxiety. He was afraid that they might be jealous of his play and become aggressive toward him. The situation which he himself had created by being so good at

[1] Freud, *New Introductory Lectures on Psycho-Analysis* (1933, pp. 118-119).

games and which had at first been a source of pleasure had now become a source of anxiety. The same theme reappeared soon afterward in a fantasy which he had when going to sleep. He thought he saw the other boys trying to knock his feet off with a large football. It came hurtling toward him and he jerked his feet up in bed in order to save them. We had already found out in this little boy's analysis that the feet had a peculiar significance for him. By the roundabout way of olfactory impressions and the ideas of stiffness and lameness they had come to represent the penis. The dream and the fantasy checked his passion for games. His play fell off and he soon lost the admiration which it had won for him at school. The meaning of this retreat was, "There's no need for you to knock my feet off, for anyhow I am no good at games now."

But the process did not end with the restriction of his ego in one direction. When he gave up games, he suddenly developed quite another side of his powers, namely, a bent which he had always had for literature and for writing compositions of his own. He used to read me poems, some of which he composed himself, and he brought me short stories, written when he was only seven, and made ambitious plans for a literary career. The footballer was transformed into an author. During one of the analytic sessions at this period he made a graph to show his attitude to the various masculine professions and hobbies. In the middle was a large thick point, which stood for literature, and in a circle round it were the different sciences, while the practical callings were indicated by more remote points. In one of the top corners of the page, close to the edge, there was a tiny little point. This stood for sport, which but a short time ago had occupied such a large place in his mind. The little point was meant to indicate the supreme contempt which he now felt for games. It was instructive to see how, in a few days' time, by a process resembling rationalization, his conscious evaluation of various activities had been influenced by his anxiety. His literary achievements at this time were really astonishing. When he ceased to be good at games, a gap was left in the functioning of his ego and this was filled by a superabundance of production in another direction. As we should expect, analysis showed that a reactivation of his rivalry with his father was responsible for his acute anxiety at the thought that the bigger boys might revenge themselves upon him.

A little girl of ten went to her first dance, full of delightful anticipation. She fancied herself in her new frock and shoes, upon which she had expended much thought, and she fell in love at first sight with the handsomest and most distinguished-looking boy at the party. It happened that, although he was a total stranger, he had the same surname as she, and around this fact she wove a fantasy that there was a secret bond between them. She made advances to him but met with no encouragement. In fact, when they were dancing together, he teased her about her clumsiness. This disappointment was at once a shock and a humiliation. From that time on she avoided parties, lost her interest in dress, and would take no trouble to learn to dance. For a little while she took some pleasure in watching other children dance, when she would look on gravely without joining in, refusing any invitations to dance herself. Gradually she came to regard all this side of her life with supreme contempt. But, like the little football player, she compensated herself for this restriction on her ego. Having given up feminine interests, she set herself to excel intellectually and in this roundabout way she finally won the respect of a number of boys of her own age. It came out later in analysis that the rebuff she had suffered from the boy with the same name as her own had meant for her the repetition of a traumatic experience of early infancy. The element in the situation from which her ego took flight was, as in the earlier cases which I have quoted, not anxiety or a sense of guilt but the intense unpleasure caused by unsuccessful competition.

Let us now return to the difference between inhibition and restriction of the ego. A person suffering from a neurotic inhibition is defending himself against the translation into action of some prohibited instinctual impulse, i.e., against the liberation of unpleasure through some internal danger. Even when, as in phobias, the anxiety and the defense seem to relate to the outside world, he is really afraid of his own inner processes. He avoids walking in the streets, in order not to be exposed to temptations which formerly assailed him. He keeps out of the way of his anxiety animal, in order to protect himself, not against the animal itself but against the aggressive tendencies within him which an encounter with it might arouse and against their consequences. In ego restriction, on the other hand, disagreeable external impressions in the present are warded off, because they might result in the revival of similar impressions from the past. Reverting to our comparison between the mechanisms of repression and denial we shall say that the difference between inhibition and ego restriction is that in the former the ego is defending itself against its own inner processes and in the latter against external stimuli.

From this fundamental distinction there ensue other differences between these two psychic situations. Behind every neurotically inhibited activity there lies an instinctual wish. The obstinacy with which each separate id impulse sets itself to attain its goal transforms the simple process of inhibition into a fixed neurotic symptom, which represents a perpetual conflict between the wish of the id and the defense set up by the ego. The patient exhausts his energy in the struggle; his id impulses adhere with but little modification to the wish to calculate, to speak in public, to play the violin or whatever it may be, while at the same time the ego with equal persistence prevents or at least mars the execution of his wish.

When restriction of the ego takes place in consequence of objective anxiety or unpleasure, there is no such fixation to the interrupted activity. The stress here falls not on the activity itself but on the unpleasure or pleasure which it produces. In its pursuit of the latter and its efforts to avoid the former the ego makes what use it pleases of all its abilities. It drops the activities which liberate unpleasure or anxiety, and has no further desire to engage in them. Whole fields of interest are abandoned and, when the ego's experience has been unfortunate, it will throw all its energies into some pursuit of an entirely opposite character. We have instances of this in the little football player who took to literature and the little dancer whose disappointment led to her becoming a prize scholar. Of course, in these cases the ego does not create new capacities; it merely makes use of those which it already possesses.

As a method of avoiding unpleasure, ego restriction, like the various forms of denial, does not come under the heading of the psychology of neurosis but is a normal stage in the development of the ego. When the ego is young and plastic, its withdrawal from one field of activity is sometimes compensated for by excellence in another, upon which it concentrates. But, when it has become rigid or has already acquired an intolerance of unpleasure and so is obsessionally fixated to the method of flight, such withdrawal is punished by impaired development. By abandoning one position after another it becomes one-sided, loses too many interests, and can show but a meager achievement.

In the theory of education the importance of the infantile ego's determination to avoid unpleasure has not been sufficiently appreciated, and this has contributed to the failure of a number of educational experiments in recent years. The modern method is to give to the growing ego of the child a greater liberty of action, above all, to allow it freely to choose its activities and interests. The idea is that thus the ego will develop better and sublimation in various forms will be achieved. But children in the latency period may attach more importance to the avoidance of anxiety and unpleasure than to direct or indirect gratification of instinct. In many cases, if they lack external guidance, their choice of occupation is determined not by their particular gifts and capacities for sublimation but by the hope of securing themselves as quickly as may be from anxiety and unpleasure. To the surprise of the educator the result of this freedom of choice is, in such cases, not the blossoming of personality but the impoverishment of the ego.

Such measures of defense against objective unpleasure and danger as the three which I have used as illustrations in this chapter represent the infantile ego's prophylaxis of neurosis—a prophylaxis which it undertakes at its peril. In order to avoid suffering, it checks the development of anxiety and inflicts deformities upon itself. Moreover, the protective measures which it adopts—whether it be flight from physi-

cal prowess to intellectual achievement, or the fixed determination of a woman to be on an equal footing with men,
or the restriction of activity to intercourse with people
weaker than the subject himself—are exposed in later life
to every kind of assault from without. The individual may
have to change his way of life because of some disaster,
such as the loss of a love object, sickness, poverty or war,
and then the ego finds itself once more confronted with the
original anxiety situations. The loss of the customary protection against anxiety may, like the frustration of some
habitual instinctual gratification, be the immediate cause of
a neurosis.

Children are still so dependent on other people that such
occasions for the formation of neurosis may be supplied or
removed as it happens to suit their elders. A child who
does not learn anything at a school where the free method
is practiced but spends his time merely looking on or drawing becomes "inhibited" under a stricter regime. Rigid insistence by other people on some disagreeable activity may
cause him to become fixated to it, but the fact that he
cannot avoid the unpleasure forces him to look around for
new means of mastering it. On the other hand, even a fully
developed inhibition or symptom may be modified if external protection is given. A mother whose anxiety is
aroused and whose pride is mortified when she sees her
child's abnormality will protect him and guard against his
encountering disagreeable external situations. But this
means that her attitude toward his symptom is precisely
that of the phobic patient to his anxiety attacks: by artificially restricting his liberty of action she enables her child
to take flight and to avoid suffering. This joint effort of
mother and child to secure the latter against anxiety and

unpleasure probably accounts for the absence of symptoms which is so common a feature in infantile neurosis. In such cases it is impossible to form an objective judgment of the extent of a child's symptoms until he has been deprived of his protection.

Part III

EXAMPLES OF TWO TYPES OF DEFENSE

CHAPTER 9

Identification with the
Aggressor

It is comparatively easy to discover the defense mechanisms
to which the ego habitually resorts, so long as each is employed separately and only in conflict with some specific
danger. When we find denial, we know that it is a reaction
to external danger; when repression takes place, the ego is
struggling with instinctual stimuli. The strong outward resemblance between inhibition and ego restriction makes it
less certain whether these processes are part of an external
or an internal conflict. The matter is still more intricate
when defensive measures are combined or when the same
mechanism is employed sometimes against an internal and
sometimes against an external force. We have an excellent
illustration of both these complications in the process of
identification. Since it is one of the factors in the development of the superego, it contributes to the mastery of instinct. But, as I hope to show in what follows, there are

occasions when it combines with other mechanisms to form one of the ego's most potent weapons in its dealings with external objects which arouse its anxiety.

August Aichhorn relates that, when he was giving advice on a child guidance committee, he had to deal with the case of a boy at an elementary school, who was brought to him because of a habit of making faces. The master complained that the boy's behavior, when he was blamed or reproved, was quite abnormal. On such occasions he made faces which caused the whole class to burst out laughing. The master's view was that either the boy was consciously making fun of him or else the twitching of his face must be due to some kind of tic. His report was at once corroborated, for the boy began to make faces during the consultation, but, when master, pupil, and psychologist were together, the situation was explained. Observing the two attentively, Aichhorn saw that the boy's grimaces were simply a caricature of the angry expression of the teacher and that, when he had to face a scolding by the latter, he tried to master his anxiety by involuntarily imitating him. The boy identified himself with the teacher's anger and copied his expression as he spoke, though the imitation was not recognized. Through his grimaces he was assimilating himself to or identifying himself with the dreaded external object.

My readers will remember the case of the little girl who tried by means of magic gestures to get over the mortification associated with her penis envy. This child was purposely and consciously making use of a mechanism to which the boy resorted involuntarily. At home she was afraid to cross the hall in the dark, because she had a dread of seeing ghosts. Suddenly, however, she hit on a device which enabled her to do it: she would run across the hall, making all sorts of peculiar gestures as she went. Before long, she triumphantly told her little brother the secret of how she had got over her anxiety. "There's no need to be afraid in the hall," she said, "you just have to pretend that you're the ghost who might meet you." This shows that her magic gestures represented the movements which she imagined ghosts would make.

We might be inclined to regard this kind of conduct as an idiosyncrasy in the two children whose cases I have quoted, but it is really one of the most natural and widespread modes of behavior on the part of the primitive ego and has long been familiar to those who have made a study of primitive methods of invoking and exorcizing spirits and of primitive religious ceremonies. Moreover, there are many children's games in which through the metamorphosis of the subject into a dreaded object anxiety is converted into pleasurable security. Here is another angle from which to study the games of impersonation which children love to play.

Now the physical imitation of an antagonist represents the assimilation of only one part of a composite anxiety experience. We learn from observation that the other elements also have to be mastered.

The six-year-old patient to whom I have several times alluded had to pay a series of visits to a dentist. At first everything went splendidly; the treatment did not hurt him and he was triumphant and made merry over the idea of anyone's being afraid of the dentist. But there came a time when my little patient arrived at my house in an extremely bad temper. The dentist had just hurt him. He was cross and unfriendly and vented his feelings on the things in my room. His first victim was a piece of India rubber. He wanted me to give it to him and, when I refused, he took a knife and tried to cut it in half. Next, he coveted a large ball of string. He wanted me to give him that too and painted me a vivid picture of what a good leash it would make for his animals. When I refused to give him the whole ball, he took the knife again and secured a large piece of the string. But he did not use it; instead, he began after a few minutes to cut it into tiny pieces. Finally, he threw away the string too, turned his attention to some pencils, and went on indefatigably sharpening them, breaking off the points, and sharpening them again. It would not be correct to say that he was playing at "dentists." There was no actual impersonation of the dentist. The child was identifying himself not with the person of the aggressor but with his aggression.

On another occasion this little boy came to me just after he had had a slight accident. He had been joining in an outdoor game at school and had run full tilt against the fist of the games master, which the latter happened to be holding up in front of him. My little patient's lip was bleeding and his face tear-stained, and he tried to conceal both facts by putting up his hand as a screen. I endeavored to comfort and reassure him. He was in a woebegone condition when he left me, but next day he appeared holding himself very erect and dressed in full armor. On his head he wore a military cap and he had a toy sword at his side and a pistol in his hand. When he saw my surprise at this transformation, he simply said, "I just wanted to have these things on when I was playing with you." He did not, however, play; instead, he sat down and wrote a letter to his mother: "Dear Mummy, please, please, please, please send me the pocketknife you promised me and don't wait till Easter!" Here again we cannot say that, in order to master the anxiety experience of the previous day, he was impersonating the teacher with whom he had collided. Nor, in this instance, was he imitating the latter's aggression. The weapons and armor, being manly attributes, evidently symbolized the teacher's strength and, like the attributes of the father in 'the animal fantasies, helped the child to identify himself with the masculinity of the adult and so to defend himself against narcissistic mortification or actual mishaps.

The examples which I have so far cited illustrate a process with which we are quite familiar. A child introjects some characteristic of an anxiety object and so assimilates an anxiety experience which he has just undergone. Here, the mechanism of identification or introjection is combined with a second important mechanism. By impersonating the aggressor, assuming his attributes or imitating his aggression, the child transforms himself from the person threatened into the person who makes the threat. In *Beyond the Pleasure Principle* (1920) the significance of this change from the passive to the active role as a means of assimilating unpleasant or traumatic experiences in infancy is discussed in detail: "If the doctor looks down a child's throat or carries out some small operation, we may be quite sure that these frightening experiences will be the subject of the next game; but we must not in that connection overlook the fact that there is a yield of pleasure from another source. As the child passes over from the passivity of the experience to the activity of the game, he hands on the disagreeable experience to one of his playmates and in this way revenges himself on a substitute" (p. 17).

What is true of play is equally true of other behavior in children. In the cases of the boy who made faces and the little girl who practiced magic, it is not clear what finally became of the threat with which they identified themselves, but in the other little boy's ill temper the aggression taken over from the dentist and the games master was directed against the world at large.

This process of transformation strikes us as more curious when the anxiety relates not to some event in the past but to something expected in the future. I remember a boy who had the habit of furiously pealing the bell of the children's home where he lived. As soon as the door was opened, he would scold the housemaid loudly for being so slow and not listening for the bell. In the interval between pulling the bell and flying into a rage he experienced anxiety lest he should be reproved for his lack of consideration in ringing so loudly. He upbraided the servant before she had time to complain of his conduct. The vehemence with which he scolded her—a prophylactic measure—indicated the intensity of his anxiety. The aggressiveness which he assumed was turned against the actual person from whom he expected aggression and not against some substitute. The reversal of the roles of attacker and attacked was in this case carried to its logical conclusion.

Jenny Waelder has given a vivid picture of this process in a five-year-old boy whom she treated.[1] When his analysis was about to touch on the material connected with masturbation and the fantasies associated with it, this little boy, who was usually shy and inhibited, became fiercely aggressive. His habitually passive attitude disappeared and there was no trace left of his feminine characteristics. In the analytic hour he pretended to be a roaring lion and attacked

[1] Presented at the Vienna Seminar on child analysis (see Hall, 1946).

the analyst. He carried a rod about with him and played at
"Krampus,"[2] i.e., he laid about him with it on the stairs, in
his own house, and in my room. His grandmother and
mother complained that he tried to strike them in the
face. His mother's uneasiness reached its climax when he
took to brandishing kitchen knives. Analysis showed that
the child's aggressiveness could not be construed as indi-
cating that some inhibition on his instinctual impulses had
been lifted. The release of his masculine tendencies was
still a long way off. He was simply suffering from anxiety.
The bringing into consciousness and the necessary confes-
sion of his former and recent sexual activities aroused in
him the expectation of punishment. According to his experience, grown-up people were angry when they discovered
a child indulging in such practices. They shouted at him,
checked him sharply with a box on the ears or beat him
with a rod; perhaps they would even cut off some part of
him with a knife. When my little patient assumed the
active role, roaring like a lion and laying about him with
the rod and the knife, he was dramatizing and forestalling
the punishment which he feared. He had introjected the
aggression of the adults in whose eyes he felt guilty and,
having exchanged the passive for the active part, he directed
his own aggressive acts against those same people. Every
time that he found himself on the verge of communicating
to me what he regarded as dangerous material, his aggressiveness increased. But directly his forbidden thoughts and
feelings broke through and had been discussed and interpreted, he felt no further need of the "Krampus" rod, which
till then he had constantly carried about with him, and he

[2] A devil who accompanied St. Nicholas and punished naughty
children.—*Translator's note.*

left it at my house. His compulsion to beat other people disappeared simultaneously with his anxious expectation of being beaten himself.

In "identification with the aggressor" we recognize a by no means uncommon stage in the normal development of the superego. When the two boys whose cases I have just described identified themselves with their elders' threats of punishment, they were taking an important step toward the formation of that institution: they were internalizing other people's criticisms of their behavior. When a child constantly repeats this process of internalization and introjects the qualities of those responsible for his upbringing, making their characteristics and opinions his own, he is all the time providing material from which the superego may take shape. But at this point children are not quite whole-hearted in acknowledging that institution. The internalized criticism is not yet immediately transformed into self-criticism. As we have seen in the examples which I have given, it is dissociated from the child's own reprehensible activity and turned back on the outside world. By means of a new defensive process identification with the aggressor is succeeded by an active assault on the outside world.

Here is a more complicated example, which will perhaps throw light on this new development in the defensive process. A certain boy, when his oedipus complex was at its height, employed this particular mechanism to master his fixation to his mother. His happy relations with her were disturbed by outbursts of resentment. He would upbraid her passionately and on all sorts of grounds, but one mysterious accusation invariably recurred: he persistently complained of her curiosity. It is easy to see the first step in the working over of his prohibited affects. In his fantasy his mother knew of his libidinal feeling for her and indignantly rejected his advances. Her indignation was actively reproduced in his own fits of resentment against her. In contrast to Jenny Waelder's patient, however, he did not reproach her on general grounds but on the specific ground of curiosity. Analysis showed that this curiosity was an element not in his mother's instinctual life but in his own. Of all the component instincts which entered into his relation with her, his scoptophilic impulse was the most difficult to master. The reversal of roles was complete. He assumed his mother's indignation and, in exchange, ascribed to her his own curiosity.

In certain phases of resistance a young patient used bitterly to reproach her analyst with being secretive. She complained that the analyst was too reserved and she would torment her with questions on personal matters and be miserable when she received no answer. Then the reproaches would cease, only to begin again after a short time, always in the same stereotyped and, as it seemed, automatic fashion. In this case again we can detect two phases in the psychic process. From time to time, because of a certain inhibition which prevented her speaking out, the patient herself consciously suppressed some very private material. She knew that she was thereby breaking the fundamental rule of analysis and she expected the analyst to rebuke her. She introjected the fantasied rebuke and, adopting the active role, applied the accusation to the analyst. Her phases of aggression exactly coincided in time with her phases of secretiveness. She criticized the analyst for the very fault of which she herself was guilty. Her own secretive behavior was perceived as reprehensible conduct on the analyst's part.

Another young patient used periodically to have fits of violent aggressiveness. I myself, her parents, and other people in less close relation with her were almost equally the objects of her resentment. There were two things in particular of which she constantly complained. First, during these phases she always had the feeling that people were keeping from her some secret which everybody knew but herself, and she was tormented by the desire to find out what it was. Secondly, she felt deeply disappointed by the shortcomings of all her friends. Just as, in the case which I last quoted, the periods in which the patient kept back material coincided with those in which she complained of secretiveness in the analyst, so this patient's aggressive phases set in automatically whenever her repressed masturbation fantasies, of which she herself was unaware, were about to emerge into consciousness. Her strictures on her love objects corresponded to the blame which she expected from them because of her masturbation in childhood. She identified herself fully with this condemnation and turned it back upon the outside world. The secret which everybody kept from her was the secret of her own masturbation, which she kept not only from others but from herself. Here again, the patient's aggressiveness corresponded to that of other people and their "secret" was a reflection of her own repression.

These three examples have given us some idea of the origin of this particular phase in the development of the function of the superego. Even when the external criticism has been introjected, the threat of punishment and the offense committed have not yet been connected up in the patient's mind. The moment the criticism is internalized, the offense is externalized. This means that the mechanism of identification with the aggressor is supplemented by another defensive measure, namely, the projection of guilt.

An ego which with the aid of the defense mechanism of projection develops along this particular line introjects the authorities to whose criticism it is exposed and incorporates them in the superego. It is then able to project the prohibited impulses outward. Its intolerance of other people precedes its severity toward itself. It learns what is regarded as blameworthy but protects itself by means of this defense mechanism from unpleasant self-criticism. Vehement indignation at someone else's wrongdoing is the precursor of and substitute for guilty feelings on its own account. Its indignation increases automatically when the perception of its own guilt is imminent. This stage in the development of the superego is a kind of preliminary phase of morality. True morality begins when the internalized criticism, now embodied in the standard exacted by the superego, coincides with the ego's perception of its own fault. From that moment, the severity of the superego is turned inward instead of outward and the subject becomes less intolerant of other people. But, when once it has reached this stage in its development, the ego has to endure the more acute unpleasure occasioned by self-criticism and the sense of guilt.

It is possible that a number of people remain arrested at the intermediate stage in the development of the superego and never quite complete the internalization of the critical process. Although perceiving their own guilt, they continue to be peculiarly aggressive in their attitude to other people. In such cases the behavior of the superego toward others is as ruthless as that of the superego toward the patient's own ego in melancholia. Perhaps when the evolution of the superego is thus inhibited, it indicates an abortive beginning of the development of melancholic states

"Identification with the aggressor" represents, on the one hand, a preliminary phase of superego development and, on the other, an intermediate stage in the development of paranoia. It resembles the former in the mechanism of identification and the latter in that of projection. At the same time, identification and projection are normal activities of the ego and their results vary greatly according to the material upon which they are employed.

The particular combination of introjection and projection to which we have applied the term "identification with the aggressor" can be regarded as normal only so long as the ego employs this mechanism in its conflict with authority, i.e., in its efforts to deal with anxiety objects. It is a defensive process which ceases to be innocuous and becomes pathological when it is carried over into a person's love life. When a husband displaces onto his wife his own impulses to be unfaithful and then reproaches her passionately with unfaithfulness, he is really introjecting her reproaches and projecting part of his own id.[3] His intention, however, is to protect himself not against aggression from without but against the shattering of his positive libidinal fixation to her by disturbing forces from within. Accordingly the result is different. Instead of an aggressive attitude toward some former external assailants the patient develops an obsessional fixation to his wife, which takes the form of projected jealousy.

When the mechanism of projection is employed as a

[3] Cf. "Some Neurotic Mechanisms in Jealousy, Paranoia and Homosexuality" (Freud, 1922, p. 223).

defense against homosexual love impulses, it is combined with yet other mechanisms. Reversal (in this case the reversal of love into hate) completes what introjection and projection have begun, and the result is the development of paranoid delusions. In either case—defense against heterosexual or against homosexual love impulses—the projection is no longer arbitrary. The ego's choice of a billet for its own unconscious impulses is determined by "the perceptual material which betrays unconscious impulses of the same kind in the partner."[4]

From the theoretical standpoint, analysis of the process of "identification with the aggressor" assists us to differentiate the various modes in which the specific defense mechanisms are employed; in practice, it enables us to distinguish in the transference anxiety attacks from outbursts of aggression. When analysis brings into the patient's consciousness genuine, unconscious, aggressive impulses, the dammed-up affect will seek relief through abreaction in the transference. But, if his aggression is due to his identifying himself with what he supposed to be our criticism, it will not be in the least affected by his "giving it practical expression" and "abreacting" it. As long as the unconscious impulses are prohibited, it increases, and it vanishes, as in the case of the little boy who confessed his masturbation, only when the dread of punishment and of the superego has been dissipated.

[4] *Ibid.*, p. 224.

CHAPTER 10

A Form of Altruism

The effect of the mechanism of projection is to break the connection between the ideational representatives of dangerous instinctual impulses and the ego. In this it resembles most closely the process of repression. Other defensive processes, such as displacement, reversal or turning round upon the self, affect the instinctual process itself: repression and projection merely prevent its being perceived. In repression the objectionable idea is thrust back into the id, while in projection it is displaced into the outside world. Another point in which projection resembles repression is that it is not associated with any particular anxiety situation but may be motivated equally by objective anxiety, superego anxiety, and instinctual anxiety. Writers of the English school of psychoanalysis maintain that in the earliest months of life, before any repression has taken place, the infant already projects its first aggressive impulses and that this process is of crucial importance for the picture which the child forms of the world around him and the way in which his personality develops.

At all events the use of the mechanism of projection is quite natural to the ego of little children throughout the earliest period of development. They employ it as a means of repudiating their own activities and wishes when these become dangerous and of laying the responsibility for them at the door of some external agent. A "strange child," an animal, even inanimate objects are all equally useful to the infantile ego for the purpose of disposing of its own faults. It is normal for it constantly to get rid of prohibited impulses and wishes in this way, handing them over in full measure to other people. If these wishes entail punishment by authorities, the ego puts forward as whipping boys the persons upon whom it has projected them; if, on the other hand, the projection was prompted by a sense of guilt, instead of criticizing itself it accuses others. In either case it dissociates itself from its proxies and is excessively intolerant of its judgment of them.

The mechanism of projection disturbs our human relations when we project our own jealousy and attribute to other people our own aggressive acts. But it may work in another way as well, enabling us to form valuable positive attachments and so to consolidate our relations with one another. This normal and less conspicuous form of projection might be described as "altruistic surrender"[1] of our own instinctual impulses in favor of other people.

The following is an example of what I mean.

A young governess reported in her analysis that, as a child, she was possessed by two ideas: she wanted to have

---

[1] *"Altruistische Abtretung."* This term was coined by Edward Bibring.

beautiful clothes and a number of children. In her fantasies she was almost obsessionally absorbed in picturing the fulfillment of these two wishes. But there were a great many other things that she demanded as well: she wished to have and to do everything that her much older playmates had and did—indeed, she wanted to do everything better than they and to be admired for her cleverness. Her everlasting cry of "Me too!" was a nuisance to her elders. It was characteristic of her desires that they were at once urgent and insatiable.

What chiefly struck one about her as an adult was her unassuming character and the modesty of the demands which she made on life. When she came to be analyzed, she was unmarried and childless and her dress was rather shabby and inconspicuous. She showed little sign of envy or ambition and would compete with other people only if she were forced to do so by external circumstances. One's first impression was that, as so often happens, she had developed in exactly the opposite direction from what her childhood would have led one to expect and that her wishes had been repressed and replaced in consciousness by reaction formations (unobtrusiveness instead of a craving for admiration and unassumingness instead of ambition). One would have expected to find that the repression was caused by a prohibition of sexuality, extending from her exhibitionistic impulses and the desire for children to the whole of her instinctual life.

But there were features in her behavior at the time when I knew her which contradicted this impression. When her life was examined in more detail, it was clear that her original wishes were affirmed in a manner which seemed scarcely possible if repression had taken place. The repudiation of her own sexuality did not prevent her from taking an affectionate interest in the love life of her women friends and colleagues. She was an enthusiastic matchmaker and many love affairs were confided to her. Although she took no trouble about her own dress, she displayed a lively interest in her friends' clothes. Childless herself, she was devoted to other people's children, as was indicated by her choice of a profession. She might be said to display an unusual degree of concern about her friends' having pretty clothes, being admired, and having children. Similarly, in spite of her own retiring behavior, she was ambitious for the men whom she loved and followed their careers with the utmost interest. It looked as if her own life had been emptied of interests and wishes; up to the time of her analysis it was almost entirely uneventful. Instead of exerting herself to achieve any aims of her own, she expended all her energy in sympathizing with the experiences of people she cared for. She lived in the lives of other people, instead of having any experience of her own.

The analysis of her infantile relations to her mother and father revealed clearly the nature of the inner transformation which had taken place. Her early renunciation of instinct had resulted in the formation of an exceptionally severe superego, which made it impossible for her to gratify her own wishes. Her penis wish, with its offshoots in the shape of ambitious masculine fantasies, was prohibited, so too her feminine wish for children and the desire to display herself, naked or in beautiful clothes, to her father, and to win his admiration. But these impulses were not repressed: she found some proxy in the outside world to serve as a repository for each of them. The vanity of her women friends provided, as it were, a foothold for the projection of her own vanity, while her libidinal wishes and ambitious fantasies were likewise deposited in the outside world. She projected her prohibited instinctual impulses onto other people, just as the patients did whose cases I quoted in the last chapter. The only difference lay in the way in which these impulses were subsequently dealt with. The patient did not dissociate herself from her proxies but identified herself with them. She showed her sympathy with their wishes and felt that there was an extraordinarily strong bond between these people and herself. Her superego, which condemned a particular instinctual impulse when it related to her own ego, was surprisingly tolerant of it in other people. She gratified her instincts by sharing in the gratification of others, employing for this purpose the mechanisms of projection and identification.[2] The retiring attitude which the prohibition of her impulses caused her to adopt where she herself was concerned vanished when it was a question of fulfilling the same wishes after they had been projected onto someone else. The surrender of her instinctual impulses in favor of other people had thus an egoistic significance, but in her efforts to gratify the impulses of others her behavior could only be called altruistic.

This passing on of her own wishes to other people was characteristic of her whole life and could be traced very clearly in the analysis of little isolated incidents. For instance, at the age of thirteen she secretly fell in love with a friend of her elder sister who had formerly been the special object of her jealousy. She had an idea that, at times, he preferred her to her sister and she was always hoping that he would give some sign of loving her. On one occasion it

[2] Compare in this connection Paul Federn's notion (1936) of "sympathetic" identification and his remarks on this subject.

happened, as it had often happened before, that she found herself slighted. The young man called unexpectedly one evening to take her sister for a walk. In analysis the patient remembered perfectly distinctly how, from having been at first paralyzed with disappointment, she suddenly began to bustle about, fetching things to make her sister "pretty" for her outing and eagerly helping her to get ready. While doing this, the patient was blissfully happy and quite forgot that it was not she, but her sister, who was going out to enjoy herself. She had projected her own desire for love and her craving for admiration onto her rival and, having identified herself with the object of her envy, she enjoyed the fulfillment of her desire.

She went through the same process when frustration rather than fulfillment was in question. She loved to give the children of whom she was in charge good things to eat. On one occasion a mother refused to give up a particular tit-bit for her child. Although the patient herself was, in general, indifferent to the pleasures of the table, the mother's refusal made her furiously indignant. She experienced the frustration of the child's wish as if it were her own, just as in the other case she had rejoiced vicariously in the fulfillment of her sister's desires. It is plain that what she had made over to other people was the right to have her wishes fulfilled without hindrance.

The last trait comes out even more clearly in the experiences of another patient of the same type. A young woman, whose relation to her father-in-law was a particularly friendly one, reacted very strangely to the death of her mother-in-law. The patient, with other women of the family, undertook to dispose of the dead woman's clothes. Unlike all the others, my patient refused to take even a single garment for her own use. Instead, she set aside one coat as a present for a cousin who was badly off. The mother-in-law's sister wanted to cut off the fur collar of the coat and keep it herself, whereupon the patient, who so far had been quite indifferent and uninterested, flew into a blind rage. She turned the full fury of her usually inhibited aggression upon her aunt and insisted on her protégée's having what she had intended for her. Analysis of this incident showed that the patient's sense of guilt prevented her from appropriating anything which had belonged to her mother-in-law. To take a garment symbolized to her the gratifying of her wish to fill her mother-in-law's place with her father-in-law. She therefore renounced any claim herself and surrendered in favor of her cousin the desire to be her "mother's" successor. Having done so, however, she felt the full force of the wish and its disappointment and was able to insist on its fulfillment, a thing which she could never do when she herself was concerned. The superego, which took up so implacable an attitude toward her own instinctual impulse, assented to the desire when it was no longer associated with the patient's own ego. When the fulfillment of another person's wish was in question, the aggressive behavior which was usually inhibited suddenly became ego syntonic.

Any number of cases similar to those which I have quoted can be observed in everyday life, when once our attention has been called to this combination of projection and identification for purposes of defense. For instance, a young girl, who had scruples of conscience about marrying herself, did all she could to encourage her sister's engagement. A patient, who suffered from obsessional inhibitions in spending any money on herself, had no hesitation in spending lavishly on presents. Another patient, who was prevented by anxiety from carrying out her plans for travel, was quite unexpectedly pressing in her advice to her friends to do so. In all these cases the patient's identification of herself with a sister, a friend, or the recipient of a gift betrayed itself by a sudden warm sense of a bond between them, which lasted as long as her own wish was being vicariously fulfilled. Jokes about "matchmaking old maids" and "meddlesome onlookers, for whom no stakes are too high"[3] are perennial. The surrender of one's own wishes to another person and the attempt to secure their fulfillment thus vicariously are, indeed, comparable to the interest and pleasure with which one watches a game in which one has no stake oneself.

This defensive process serves two purposes. On the one hand it enables the subject to take a friendly interest in the gratification of other people's instincts and so, indirectly and in spite of the superego's prohibition, to gratify his own, while, on the other, it liberates the inhibited activity and aggression primarily designed to secure the fulfillment of the instinctual wishes in their original relation to himself. The patient who could not lift a finger to gratify her own oral impulses could feel indignant at the mother's refusal to indulge her child, i.e., at oral renunciation imposed on someone else. The daughter-in-law who was prohibited from claiming the rights of the dead wife felt it permissible to defend the symbolic right of another with the full force of her aggression. An employee who would never venture to ask for a raise in salary for herself suddenly besieged the manageress with demands that one of her fellow workers should have her rights. Analysis of such situations shows

[3] *"Kiebitze, denen kein Spiel zu hoch ist."*

that this defensive process has its origin in the infantile conflict with parental authority about some form of instinctual gratification. Aggressive impulses against the mother, prohibited so long as it is a question of fulfilling the subject's own wishes, are given rein when the wishes are ostensibly those of someone else. The most familiar representative of this type of person is the public benefactor, who with the utmost aggressiveness and energy demands money from one set of people in order to give it to another. Perhaps the most extreme instance is that of the assassin who, in the name of the oppressed, murders the oppressor. The object against which the liberated aggression is directed is invariably the representative of the authority which imposed renunciation of instinct on the subject in infancy.

Various factors determine the selection of the object in favor of whom instinctual impulses are surrendered. Possibly the perception of the prohibited impulse in another person is sufficient to suggest to the ego that here is an opportunity for projection. In the case of the patient who assisted in the disposal of her mother-in-law's property, the fact that the vicarious figure was not a near relation was a guarantee of the harmlessness of the wish which, when cherished by the patient herself, represented her incestuous impulses. In most cases the substitute has once been the object of envy. The altruistic governess in my first example displaced her ambitious fantasies onto her men friends and her libidinal wishes onto her women friends. The former succeeded to her affection for her father and her big brother, both of whom had been the object of her penis envy, while the latter represented the sister upon whom, at a rather later period of childhood, that envy was displaced in the form of envy of her beauty. The patient felt that the fact that she was a girl prevented her from achieving her ambitions and, at the same time, that she was not even a pretty enough girl really to be attractive to men. In her disappointment with herself she displaced her wishes onto objects who she felt were better qualified to fulfill them. Her men friends were vicariously to achieve for her in professional life that which she herself could never achieve, and the girls who were better-looking than herself were to do the same in the sphere of love. Her altruistic surrender was a method of overcoming her narcissistic mortification.

This surrender of instinctual wishes to an object better qualified to fulfill them often determines the relation of a girl to some man whom she chooses to represent her—to the detriment of any true object relation. On the grounds of this "altruistic" attachment she expects him to carry out the projects in which she believes herself to be handicapped by her sex: for instance, she wants him to lead the life of a student or to adopt a particular profession or to become famous or rich in her place. In such cases egoism and altruism may be blended in very various proportions. We know that parents sometimes delegate to their children their projects for their own lives, in a manner at once altruistic and egoistic. It is as if they hoped through the child, whom they regard as better qualified for the purpose than themselves, to wrest from life the fulfillment of the ambitions which they themselves have failed to realize. Perhaps even the purely altruistic relation of a mother to her son is largely determined by such a surrender of her own wishes to the object whose sex makes him "better qualified" to carry them out. A man's success in life does, indeed, go far to compensate the women of his family for the renunciation of their own ambitions.

The finest and most detailed study of this altruistic surrender is to be found in Edmond Rostand's play *Cyrano de Bergerac.* The hero of the play is a historical figure, a French nobleman of the seventeenth century, a poet and officer of the Guards, famous for his intellect and valor but handicapped in his wooing of women by a peculiarly ugly nose. He falls in love with his beautiful cousin, Roxane, but, conscious of his ugliness, he at once resigns every hope of winning her. Instead of using his formidable skill as a fencer to keep all rivals at a distance, he surrenders his own aspirations to her love in favor of a man better looking than himself. Having made this renunciation, he devotes his strength, his courage, and his brains to the service of this more fortunate lover and does all he can to help him to attain his desire. The climax of the play is a scene at night, under the balcony of the woman whom both men love. Cyrano whispers to his rival the words with which to win her. Then he takes the other's place in the dark and speaks for him, forgetting in the ardor of his wooing that he himself is not the wooer and only at the last moment falling back into his attitude of surrender when the suit of Christian, the handsome lover, is accepted and he goes up to the balcony to embrace his love. Cyrano becomes more and more devoted to his rival and in battle tries to save Christian's life rather than his own. When this vicarious figure is taken from him by death, he feels that it is not permissible for him to woo Roxane. That the poet is depicting in Cyrano's "altruism" something more than a strange love adventure is clear from the parallel which he draws between Cyrano's love life and his fate as a poet. Just as Christian woos Roxane with the help of Cyrano's poems and letters, writers like Corneille, Molière, and Swift borrow whole scenes from his unknown works, thus enhancing their own fame. In the play Cyrano accepts this fate. He is as ready to lend his words to Christian, who is handsomer than himself, as to Molière, who is a greater genius. The personal defect which he thinks renders him contemptible makes him feel that the others who are preferred to himself are better qualified than he to realize his wish fantasies.

In conclusion, we may for a moment study the notion of altruistic surrender from another angle, namely, in its relation to the fear of death. Anyone who has very largely projected his instinctual impulses onto other people knows nothing of this fear. In the moment of danger his ego is not really concerned for his own life. He experiences instead excessive concern and anxiety for the lives of his love objects. Observation shows that these objects, whose safety is so vital to him, are the vicarious figures upon whom he has displaced his instinctual wishes. For instance, the young governess, whose case I have described, suffered from quite excessive anxiety about the safety of her friends in pregnancy and childbirth. Again, as is shown in the sketch which I have given, Cyrano sets Christian's safety in battle far above his own. It would be a mistake to suppose that this is a question of suppressed rivalry breaking through in death wishes, which are then warded off. Analysis shows that both the anxiety and the absence of anxiety are due rather to the subject's feeling that his own life is worth living and preserving only insofar as there is opportunity in it for the gratification of his instincts. When his impulses have been surrendered in favor of other people, their lives become precious rather than his own. The death of the vicarious figure means—as Christian's death meant for Cyrano—the destruction of all hope of fulfillment.

It was only after analysis, when she happened to fall ill, that the young governess discovered that the thought of dying was painful to her. To her own surprise she found that she ardently desired to live long enough to furnish her new home and to pass an examination which would secure her promotion in her profession. Her home and the examination signified, though in a sublimated form, the fulfillment of instinctual wishes which analysis had enabled her to relate once more to her own life.[4]

---

[4] There is an obvious similarity between the situation in altruistic surrender and the conditions which determine male homosexuality. The homosexual makes over his claim on his mother's love to a younger brother whom he has previously envied. It is true that he proceeds to satisfy this demand himself by adopting a maternal attitude, i.e., by enjoying both the active and the passive side of the relation between mother and son. It is difficult to determine how far this process contributed to the various forms of altruistic surrender which I have described. Cyrano and the altruistic young governess must both have derived pleasure from this mechanism even before they could rejoice vicariously in the successes of their substitutes. Their rapture of giving and helping shows that the surrender is in itself a gratification of instinct. As in the process of identification with the aggressor, passivity is transformed into activity, narcissistic mortification is compensated for by the sense of power associated with the role of benefactor, while the passive experience of frustration finds compensation in the active conferring of happiness on others.

It remains an open question whether there is such a thing as a genuinely altruistic relation to one's fellowmen, in which the gratification of one's own instinct plays no part at all, even in some displaced and sublimated form. In any case it is certain that projection and identification are not the only means of acquiring an attitude which has every appearance of altruism; for instance, another and easy route to the same goal is by way of the various forms of masochism.

Part IV

DEFENSE MOTIVATED BY FEAR OF THE STRENGTH OF THE INSTINCTS

Illustrated by the Phenomena of Puberty

CHAPTER **11**

The Ego and the Id
at Puberty

Of all the periods in human life in which the instinctual processes are beyond question of paramount importance, that of puberty has always attracted most attention. For a long time now the psychic phenomena which signalize the advent of sexual maturity have been the subject of psychological study. In nonanalytic writings we find many striking descriptions of the changes which take place in character during these years, of the disturbances in the psychic equilibrium, and, above all, of the incomprehensible and irreconcilable contradictions then apparent in the psychic life. Adolescents are excessively egoistic, regarding themselves as the center of the universe and the sole object of interest, and yet at no time in later life are they capable of so much self-sacrifice and devotion. They form the most passionate love relations, only to break them off as abruptly as they began them. On the one hand, they throw themselves enthusiastically into the life of the community and, on the other, they have an overpowering longing for solitude. They oscillate between blind submission to some self-chosen leader and defiant rebellion against any and every authority. They are selfish and materially minded and at the same time full of lofty idealism. They are ascetic but will suddenly plunge into instinctual indulgence of the most primitive character. At times their behavior to other people is rough and inconsiderate, yet they themselves are extremely touchy. Their moods veer between light-hearted optimism and the blackest pessimism. Sometimes they will work with indefatigable enthusiasm and at other times they are sluggish and apathetic.

Official psychology seeks to explain these phenomena in two very different ways. According to the one theory, this upheaval in the psychic life is probably due to chemical changes, i.e., it is the direct consequence of the beginning of the functioning of the sexual glands. That is to say, it is simply the psychic accompaniment of physiological changes. The other theory rejects the idea of any such connection between the physical and the psychic. According to it, the revolution which takes place in the psychic sphere is simply a sign that the individual has attained to psychic maturity, just as the simultaneous physical changes are signs of physical maturity. It is pointed out that the fact that psychic and physical processes appear simultaneously is no proof that the one group is the cause of the other. Thus the second theory claims that psychic development is entirely independent of glandular and instinctual processes. There is one single point at which these two trends of thought in psychology meet: both are agreed that not only the physical but also the psychic phenomena of puberty are of the utmost importance in the development of the individual and that here are the beginning and the root of the sexual life, of the capacity for love, and of character as a whole.

In contrast to academic psychology, psychoanalysis has hitherto shown remarkably little inclination to concentrate on the psychological problems of puberty, although in other connections it has very often taken contradictions in the psychic life as a starting point for its investigations. If we except a few works in which the foundation for a study of puberty has been laid (Freud, 1905; Jones, 1922; Bernfeld, 1923), we may say that analytic writers have rather neglected that period and devoted more attention to other stages of development. The reason is obvious. Psychoanalysis does not share the view that the sexual life of human beings begins at puberty. According to our theory, the sexual life has two starting points. It begins for the first time in the first year of life. It is in the early infantile sexual period and not at puberty that the crucial steps in development are taken, the important pregenital phases of sexual organization are passed through, the different component instincts are developed and brought into action and the normality or abnormality of the individual, his capacity or incapacity for love, are determined. We expect to derive from our study of this early period the knowledge of the origin and development of sexuality for which academic psychology seeks in its study of puberty. Puberty is merely one of the phases in the development of human life. It is the first recapitulation of the infantile sexual period; at a later period in life, a second takes place at the climacteric. Each of the sexual periods is a renewal and resuscitation of that which has gone before. In addition, of course, each contributes something of its own to human sexual life.

Owing to the fact that physical sexual maturity is attained at puberty, genitality occupies the foreground at this period and the genital trends predominate over the pregenital component instincts. At the climacteric, when there is a decline in the physical sexual functions, the genital impulses flare up for the last time and pregenital impulses come into their own again.

Hitherto psychoanalytic writings have been principally concerned with the *similarities* between these three periods of turbulent sexuality in human life. They resemble one another most closely in the quantitative relations between the strength of the ego and of the instincts. In each case—in the early infantile period, at puberty, and at the climacteric—a relatively strong id confronts a relatively weak ego. Thus we may say that they are periods in which the id is vigorous and the ego enfeebled. There is, besides, a strong qualitative similarity with respect to one of the two factors in the ego-id relation in these three periods. A man's id remains much the same throughout life. It is true that the instinctual impulses are capable of transformation when they come into collision with the ego and the demands of the outside world. But within the id itself little or no change takes place, apart from the advance made from pregenital to genital instinctual aims. The sexual wishes, which are always ready upon any reinforcement of libido to emerge from repression, and the object cathexes and fantasies associated with them alter but little in childhood, at puberty, in adult life, and at the climacteric. We see then that the qualitative resemblances between the three periods in human life in which libido is increased are due to the relative immutability of the id.

So far, psychoanalytic writers have paid less attention to

the *differences* between these periods. These differences arise from the second factor in the relation between the id and the ego, namely, the human ego's great capacity for transformation. The immutability of the id is matched by the mutability of the ego. Let us take as an example the ego in early childhood and the ego at puberty. At the one period and at the other it differs in compass, in content, in its knowledge and capacities, in its subordinate relationships and anxieties. Consequently, in its conflicts with the instincts it makes use of different defense mechanisms in the different periods. We may expect that a more detailed examination of these differences between early infancy and puberty will throw light on the formation of the ego, just as the instinctual life has been illuminated by the study of the resemblances between these periods.

As in the investigation of the instinctual processes, so in the study of the ego the later development can be understood only from the earlier. We must grasp the nature of the ego situation in early infancy, before we can explain the disturbances to which the ego is liable at puberty. In little children the conflict between ego and id has its peculiar conditions. The demands for instinctual gratification, which spring from the wishes characteristic of the oral, anal, and phallic phases, are extraordinarily urgent and the affects and fantasies associated with the oedipus complex and the castration complex are intensely vivid; the ego which confronts them is only in the process of formation and so is still weak and undeveloped. Nevertheless, a little child is not a being of unbridled instinct, nor, in ordinary circumstances, is he aware of the pressure of instinctual anxiety within him. In the external world, i.e., in the educational influences brought to bear upon him, his feeble ego has a powerful ally against his instinctual life. The situation does not arise in which the ego has to measure its own puny strength against the very much stronger instinctual impulses, to which, if left to itself, it must inevitably succumb. We hardly leave the child time to become aware of his own wishes or to estimate his own strength or weakness in relation to his instincts. The child's attitude toward the ego is simply dictated to him by the promises and threats of other people, that is to say, by the hope of love and the expectation of punishment.

Under such external influence little children, in the course of a few years, acquire a very considerable capacity for controlling their instinctual life, but it is impossible to determine how much of this achievement is to be attributed to their ego and how much to direct pressure by external forces. If in this situation of conflict the child's ego places itself on the side of the outside influences, the child is said to be "good." If it takes the part of the id and fights against the restriction of instinctual gratification which is imposed on it by education, he is "naughty." The science which has devoted itself to the detailed study of this oscillation of the infantile ego between the id and the outside world is that of pedagogy. It seeks for means to make the alliance between educational forces and the ego even closer and their common struggle for the mastery of instinct more successful.

But in little children there is also an endopsychic conflict, which is beyond the reach of education. The outside world very soon establishes a representative in the child's psyche, in the shape of objective anxiety. The occurrence of such anxiety is not in itself evidence of the formation of a higher institution—the conscience or superego—within the ego, but it is its precursor. Objective anxiety is the anticipation of suffering which may be inflicted on the child as a punishment by outside agents, a kind of "fore-pain" which governs the ego's behavior, no matter whether the expected punishment always takes place or not. On the one hand, this anxiety is acute in proportion to the dangerous or menacing behavior of those with whom the child is in contact. On the other hand, it is reinforced by the turning of instinctual processes against the self, is frequently combined with anxiety originating in fantasy, and takes no note of objective changes, so that its connection with reality becomes ever looser. It is certain that in the minds of little children urgent instinctual demands conflict with acute objective anxiety, and the symptoms of infantile neurosis are attempts at solving this conflict. The study and description of these inner struggles are debatable ground among scientists: some hold that they are the province of pedagogy, while we feel sure that they lie within the domain of the theory of the neuroses.

There is another characteristic feature in the ego situation of little children, which is never reproduced in later life. In all the later defense situations both the combatants are already present: an instinct confronts a more or less rigid ego, with which it must come to terms. But in little children the ego is the product of the conflict itself, and that side of the ego which, throughout life, will have to deal with the task of mastering the instincts only comes to birth at this early period under the combined pressure of the id's instinctual demands and that objective anxiety which is external in origin. The ego may be said to be "made to measure,"[1] i.e., nicely adapted to hold the balance between the two forces: the urge of instinct and pressure from without. We regard the first infantile period as over when this side of ego formation has reached a certain stage. The ego has taken up the position it intends to occupy in its battle with the id. It has decided what proportion of gratification and of renunciation of instinct it means to insist upon in solving its various conflicts. It has accustomed itself to a certain measure of delay in obtaining its desires. The methods of defense which it prefers bear the stamp of objective anxiety. We may say that a *modus vivendi* has been established between the id and the ego, to which, from now on, both will adhere.

In the course of a few years the situation alters. The latency period sets in, with a physiologically conditioned decline in the strength of the instincts, and a truce is called in the defensive warfare waged by the ego. It now has leisure to devote itself to other tasks, and it acquires fresh contents, knowledge, and capacities. At the same time it becomes stronger in relation to the outside world; it is less helpless and submissive and does not regard that world as quite so omnipotent as heretofore. Its whole attitude to external objects gradually changes as it surmounts the oedipus situation. Complete dependence on the parents ceases and identification begins to take the place of object love. More and more the principles held up to the child by his parents and teachers—their wishes, requirements, and ideals—are introjected. In his inner life the outside world no longer makes itself felt solely in the form of objective anxiety. He has set up within his ego a permanent institution, in which

[1] Ultramodern educational methods might be described as an attempt to make the outside world "to measure" for the child.

are embodied the demands of those around him and which we call the superego. Simultaneously with this development a change takes place in the infantile anxiety. Fear of the outside world looms less large and gradually gives place to fear of the new representatives of the old power—to super-ego anxiety, anxiety of conscience, and the sense of guilt. This means that the ego of the latency period has acquired a new ally in the struggle to master the instinctual processes. Anxiety of conscience prompts the defense against instinct in the latency period, just as it was prompted by objective anxiety in the early infantile period. As before, it is difficult to determine how much of the control over instinct ac-quired during the latency period is to be attributed to the ego itself and how much to the powerful influence of the superego.

But the breathing space provided by the latency period does not last long. The struggle between the two antago-nists, the ego and the id, has scarcely ended in this tem-porary truce before the terms of agreement are radically altered by the reinforcement of one of the combatants. The physiological process which marks the attainment of phys-ical sexual maturity is accompanied by a stimulation of the instinctual processes, which is carried over into the psychic sphere in the form of an influx of libido. The relation estab-lished between the forces of the ego and the id is destroyed, the painfully achieved psychic balance is upset, with the result that the inner conflicts between the two institutions blaze up afresh.

At first there is very little to report on the side of the id. The interval between latency and puberty—the so-called prepubertal period—is merely preparatory to physical sexual maturity. So far, no qualitative change has taken place in the instinctual life, but the quantity of instinctual energy has increased. This increase is not confined to the sexual life. There is more libido at the id's disposal and it cathects indiscriminately any id impulses which are at hand. Aggressive impulses are intensified to the point of complete unruliness, hunger becomes voracity, and the naughtiness of the latency period turns into the criminal behavior of adolescence. Oral and anal interests, long submerged, come to the surface again. Habits of cleanliness, laboriously acquired during the latency period, give place to pleasure in dirt and disorder, and instead of modesty and sympathy we find exhibitionistic tendencies, brutality and cruelty to animals. The reaction formations, which seemed to be firmly established in the structure of the ego, threaten to fall to pieces. At the same time, old tendencies which had disappeared come into consciousness. The oedipus wishes are fulfilled in the form of fantasies and daydreams, in which they have undergone but little distortion; in boys ideas of castration and in girls penis envy once more become the center of interest. There are very few new elements in the invading forces. Their onslaught merely brings once more to the surface the familiar content of the early infantile sexuality of little children.

But the infantile sexuality thus resuscitated no longer encounters the former conditions. The ego of the early infantile period was undeveloped and indeterminate, impressionable and plastic under the influence of the id; in the prepubertal period, on the contrary, it is rigid and firmly consolidated. It already knows its own mind. The infantile ego was capable of suddenly revolting against the outside world and of allying itself with the id to obtain instinctual gratification, but, if the ego of the adolescent does this, it becomes involved in conflicts with the superego. Its firmly established relation to the id on the one hand and the superego on the other—that which we call character—makes the ego unyielding. It can know but one wish: to preserve the character developed during the latency period, to re-establish the former relation between its own forces and those of the id, and to reply to the greater urgency of the instinctual demands with redoubled efforts to defend itself. In this struggle to preserve its own existence unchanged the ego is motivated equally by objective anxiety and anxiety of conscience and employs indiscriminately all the methods of defense to which it has ever had recourse in infancy and during the latency period. It represses, displaces, denies, and reverses the instincts and turns them against the self; it produces phobias and hysterical symptoms and binds anxiety by means of obsessional thinking and behavior. If we scrutinize this struggle for supremacy between the ego and the id, we realize that almost all the disquieting phenomena of the prepubertal period correspond to different phases in the conflict. Increased activity of fantasy, lapses into pregenital (i.e., perverse) sexual gratification, aggressive or criminal behavior signify partial successes of the id, while the occurrence of various forms of anxiety, the development of ascetic traits, and the accentuation of neurotic symptoms and inhibitions denote a more vigorous defense, i.e., the partial success of the ego.

With the attainment of bodily sexual maturity, the beginning of puberty proper, there is a further change, this time of a qualitative character. Hitherto the heightening of instinctual cathexis has been of a general, undifferentiated nature; now a change takes place (at any rate in the case of males), the genital impulses becoming more powerfully cathected. In the psychic sphere this means that the libidinal cathexis is withdrawn from pregenital impulses and concentrated on genital feelings, aims, and ideas of objects. Genitality acquires thereby an increased psychic importance, while the pregenital tendencies are relegated to the background. The first result is an apparent improvement in the situation. Those responsible for the education of the adolescent, who have been concerned and puzzled by the pregenital character of his instinctual life during the prepubertal period, now note with relief that the whole turmoil of boorishness, aggressiveness, and perverse behavior has vanished like a nightmare. The genital masculinity which succeeds to it meets with a far more favorable and indulgent judgment, even when it transgresses the limits of social convention. Yet this physiological, spontaneous cure of pregenitality, the result of the natural development which takes place at puberty, is largely deceptive. There may be a beneficent compensation, but only in cases hitherto characterized by quite definite pregenital fixations. For instance, a boy whose attitude has been passive and feminine will suddenly swing over to the masculine-active position when the libidinal cathexis is transferred to the genitals. But this does not mean that the castration anxiety and conflicts which gave rise to his feminine attitude have been solved or abolished. They are merely overlaid by the transitory heightening of the genital cathexis. When the pressure of the instincts, which becomes so great at puberty, sinks to its normal level in adult life, the anxiety and the conflicts will probably reappear unchanged and again interfere with his masculinity. The same is true of oral and anal fixations, which for the time being become less important during the accession of libido at puberty. Nevertheless, at

bottom they are as important as ever and the old pathogenic attraction of these pregenital formations will in later
life be just as great. Again, there can be no compensating
effect at puberty when phallic rather than oral and anal
interests have already predominated in childhood and the
prepubertal period—that is to say, in boys with a tendency
to phallic exhibitionism. In such cases the accession of
genital libido at puberty not only does not mitigate the
trouble but actually fosters it. No spontaneous cure takes
place in the infantile perversion: on the contrary, there is
an extremely disquieting accentuation of the morbid condition. The phallic tendencies are carried to such a pitch
that the patient's genital masculinity is abnormally exaggerated and becomes uncontrollable.

This estimate of the normality or abnormality of particular instinctual aims depends, however, on a standard of
values which belongs to adult life and has little or nothing
to do with the ego of the adolescent. The inner defensive
conflict goes on and not much attention is paid to these
values. In adolescence, the attitude of the ego toward the
id is primarily determined by quantitative and not by qualitative considerations. The point at issue is not the gratification or frustration of this or that instinctual wish but the
nature of the psychic structure in childhood and latency,
as a whole and in general. There are two extremes in which
the conflict may possibly end. Either the id, now grown
strong, may overcome the ego, in which case no trace will
be left of the previous character of the individual, and the
entrance into adult life will be marked by a riot of uninhibited gratification of instinct. Or the ego may be victorious, in which case the character of the individual during
the latency period will declare itself for good and all. When

this happens, the id impulses of the adolescent are confined within the narrow limits prescribed for the instinctual life of the child. No use can be made of the increased libido, and there has to be a constant expenditure on anticathexes, defense mechanisms, and symptoms in order to hold it in check. Apart from the resulting crippling of the instinctual life, the fact that the victorious ego becomes rigidly fixed is permanently injurious to the individual. Ego institutions which have resisted the onslaught of puberty without yielding generally remain throughout life inflexible, unassailable, and insusceptible of the rectification which a changing reality demands.

It would seem natural to suppose that the issue of the conflict in one or another of these extremes or its happy solution in a new agreement between the psychic institutions and, further, the many different phases through which it passes are determined by a quantitative factor, namely, the variations in the absolute strength of the instincts. But this simple explanation is contradicted by analytic observation of the processes in individuals at puberty. Of course, it is not the case that, when the instincts become stronger for physiological reasons, the individual is necessarily more at their mercy or, on the other hand, that with a decline in the strength of the instincts those psychic phenomena become more prominent in which the ego and the superego play a greater part than the id. We know from the study of neurotic symptoms and premenstrual states that, whenever the demands of instinct become more urgent, the ego is impelled to redouble its defensive activities. On the other hand, when the instinctual claims are less pressing, the danger associated with them diminishes and with it the objective anxiety, the anxiety of conscience, and the instinctual anxiety of the ego. Except in cases in which the latter is entirely submerged by the id, we find the converse of the suggested relation. Any additional pressure of instinctual demands stiffens the resistance of the ego to the instinct in question and intensifies the symptoms, inhibitions, etc., based upon that resistance, while, if the instincts become less urgent, the ego becomes more yielding and more ready to permit gratification. This means that the absolute strength of the instincts during puberty (which in any case cannot be measured or estimated independently) affords no prognosis of the final issue of puberty. The factors by which this is determined are relative: first, the strength of the id impulses, which is conditioned by the physiological process at puberty; second, the ego's tolerance or intolerance of instinct, which depends on the character formed during the latency period; third—and this is the qualitative factor which decides the quantitative conflict—the nature and efficacy of the defense mechanisms at the ego's command, which vary with the constitution of the particular individual, i.e., his disposition to hysteria or to obsessional neurosis, and with the lines upon which he has developed.

CHAPTER 12

Instinctual Anxiety During Puberty

It has always been recognized that those phases in human life during which there is an increase of libido are of immense importance for the analytic investigation of the id. Owing to the heightened cathexis, wishes, fantasies, and instinctual processes which at other periods occur unnoticed or are confined to the unconscious emerge into consciousness, surmounting, when necessary, the obstacles placed in their way by repression and becoming accessible to observation as they force their way into the open.

It is equally important to focus our attention on these periods of increased libido when we are studying the ego. As we have seen, the indirect effect of the intensification of instinctual impulses is the redoubling of the subject's efforts to master the instincts. General tendencies in the ego, which in periods of tranquillity in the instinctual life are hardly noticeable, become more clearly defined, and the well-marked ego mechanisms of the latency period or adult life may be so exaggerated as to produce a morbid distortion of character. Of the various attitudes which the ego may adopt toward the instinctual life, there are two in particular which, when thus accentuated at puberty, strike the observer with fresh force and explain some of the peculiarities typical of this period. I refer to the asceticism and the intellectuality of adolescence.

ASCETICISM AT PUBERTY

Alternating with instinctual excesses and irruptions from the id and with other, apparently contradictory, attitudes, there is sometimes in adolescence an antagonism toward the instincts which far surpasses in intensity anything in the way of repression which we are accustomed to see under normal conditions or in more or less severe cases of neurosis. In the mode of its manifestation and the width of its range it is less akin to the symptoms of pronounced neurotic disease than to the asceticism of religious fanatics. In neurosis we find that there is always a connection between the repression of an instinct and the nature or quality of the instinct repressed. Thus hysterics repress the genital impulses associated with the object wishes of the oedipus complex but are more or less indifferent or tolerant in their attitude toward other instinctual wishes, e.g., anal or aggressive impulses. Obsessional neurotics repress the anal-sadistic wishes which, in consequence of regression, have become the vehicles of their sexuality, but they tolerate oral gratification and have no particular mistrust of any exhibitionistic impulses which they may have, so long as these are not directly connected with the nucleus of their neurosis. Again, in melancholia it is the oral tendencies in particular which are repudiated, while phobic patients repress the impulses associated with the castration complex. In none of these cases is there an indiscriminate repudiation of instinct, and we always find in analyzing them that there is a definite relation between the quality of the instinct repressed and the subject's reasons for expelling it from consciousness.

A different picture meets our eyes when, in analyzing adolescents, we investigate their repudiation of instinct. It is true that, here too, the starting point of the process is to be found in those centers of instinctual life which are subject to special prohibition, e.g., the incest fantasies of the prepubertal period or the increased tendency to physical onanistic activities in which such wishes find their discharge. But from that point the process extends more or less indiscriminately over the whole of life. As I have already remarked, adolescents are not so much concerned with the gratification or frustration of specific instinctual wishes as with instinctual gratification or frustration as such. Young people who pass through the kind of ascetic phase which I have in mind seem to fear the quantity rather than the quality of their instincts. They mistrust enjoyment in general and so their safest policy appears to be simply to counter more urgent desires with more stringent prohibitions. Every time the instinct says, "I will," the ego retorts, "Thou shalt not," much after the manner of strict parents in the early training of little children. This adolescent mistrust of instinct has a dangerous tendency to spread; it may begin with instinctual wishes proper and extend to the most ordinary physical needs. We have all met young people who severely renounced any impulses which savored of sexuality and who avoided the society of those of their own age, declined to join in any entertainment, and, in true puritanical fashion, refused to have anything to do with the theater, music or dancing. We can understand that there is a connection between the forgoing of pretty and attractive clothes and the prohibition of sexuality. But we begin to be disquieted when the renunciation is extended to things which are harmless and necessary, as, for instance, when a young person denies himself the most ordinary protection against cold, mortifies the flesh in every possible way, and exposes his health to unnecessary risks, when he not only gives up particular kinds of oral enjoyment but "on principle" reduces his daily food to a minimum, when, from having enjoyed long nights of sound sleep, he forces himself to get up early, when he is reluctant to laugh or smile, or when, in extreme cases, he defers defecation and urination as long as possible, on the grounds that one ought not immediately to give way to all one's physical needs.

There is yet another point in which this sort of repudiation of instinct differs from ordinary repression. In neurosis we are accustomed to see that, whenever a particular gratification of instinct is repressed, some substitute is found for it. In hysteria this is done by conversion, i.e., the sexual excitation finds discharge in other bodily zones or processes, which have become sexualized. In obsessional neurosis there is a substitutive pleasure on the level to which regression has taken place, while in phobias there is at least some epinosic gain. Or prohibited forms of gratification are exchanged for other modes of enjoyment, through a process of displacement and reaction formation, while we know that true neurotic symptoms such as hysterical attacks, tics, obsessional actions, the habit of brooding, etc., represent compromises in which the instinctual demands of the id are no less effectively fulfilled than the dictates of the ego and the superego. But in the repudiation of instinct characteristic of adolescence no loophole is left for such substitutive gratification: the mechanism seems to be a different one. Instead of compromise formations (corresponding to neurotic symptoms) and the usual processes of displacement, regression, and turning against the self we find almost invariably a swing-over from asceticism to instinctual excess, the adolescent suddenly indulging in everything which he had previously held to be prohibited and disregarding any sort of external restrictions. On account of their antisocial character these adolescent excesses are in themselves unwelcome manifestations; nevertheless, from the analytic standpoint they represent transitory spontaneous recovery from the condition of asceticism. Where no such recovery takes place and the ego in some inexplicable way is strong enough to carry through its repudiation of instinct without any deviation, the result is a paralysis of the subject's vital activities—a kind of a catatonic condition, which can no longer be regarded as a normal phenomenon of puberty but must be recognized as a psychotic affection.

The question arises whether we are really justified in differentiating the repudiation of instinct during puberty from the usual process of repression. The basis for such a theoretical distinction is that, in the case of adolescents, the process begins with the fear of the quantity of instinct rather than of the quality of any particular impulses and ends not in substitutive gratifications and compromise formations but in an abrupt juxtaposition or succession of instinctual renunciation and instinctual excess or, as we may say more correctly, in their alternation. On the other hand, we know that in ordinary neurotic repression the quantitative cathexis of the instinct to be repressed is an important factor and that in obsessional neurosis it is quite the usual thing for prohibition and indulgence to succeed one another. Nevertheless, we still have the impression that a more primitive and less complex process is at work in the asceticism of adolescence than in repression proper; possibly the former represents a special case, or rather a preliminary phase, of repression.

Long ago the analytic study of the neuroses suggested that there is in human nature a disposition to repudiate certain instincts, in particular the sexual instincts, indiscriminately and independently of individual experience. This disposition appears to be a phylogenetic inheritance, a kind of deposit accumulated from acts of repression practiced by many generations and merely continued, not initiated, by individuals. To describe this dual attitude of mankind toward the sexual life—constitutional aversion coupled with passionate desire—Bleuler coined the term *ambivalence*.

During the calmer periods of life, the ego's primary antagonism to instinct—its dread of the strength of the instincts, as we have called it—is not much more than a theoretical concept. We conjecture that it is invariably the basis of instinctual anxiety, but for the observer it tends to be obscured by the much more conspicuous and obtrusive phenomena arising from objective anxiety or anxiety of conscience and resulting from shocks to which the individual has been exposed.

Probably the increase in the quantity of instinct at puberty and other periods in life when there is a sudden accession of instinctual energy accentuates this primary antagonism to such a degree that it becomes a specific and active defense mechanism. If this is so, the asceticism of puberty must be interpreted not as a series of repressive activities, qualitatively conditioned, but simply as a manifestation of the innate hostility between the ego and the instincts, which is indiscriminate, primary, and primitive.

INTELLECTUALIZATION AT PUBERTY

We have come to the conclusion that in periods characterized by an accession of libido general attitudes of the ego may develop into definite methods of defense. If this is so, it may explain other changes which take place in the ego at puberty.

We know that most of the transformations during this period occur in the instinctual and affective life and, further, that the ego always undergoes a secondary modification when it is directly engaged in the attempt to master the instincts and the affects. But this by no means exhausts the possibilities of change in the adolescent. With the accession of instinctual energy he becomes more a creature of instinct; that is natural and needs no further explanation. He also becomes more moral and ascetic, the explanation being that a conflict is taking place between the ego and the id. But he becomes, besides, more intelligent and all his intellectual interests are keener. At first we do not see how this advance in intellectual development is connected with the advance in the development of the instincts and with the strengthening of the ego institutions to resist the fiercer assaults launched upon it.

In general, we should expect to find that the storms of instinct or affect bore an inverse relation to the subject's intellectual activity. Even in the normal state of being in love a man's intellectual capacities tend to diminish and his reason is less reliable than usual. The more passionate his desire to fulfill his instinctual impulses, the less inclination has he as a rule to bring his intellect to bear on them and to examine their basis in reason.

It seems at first sight that in adolescence the reverse is the case. There is a type of young person whose sudden spurt in intellectual development is no less noticeable and surprising than his rapid development in other directions. We know how often the whole interest of boys during the latency period is concentrated on things which have an actual, objective existence. Some boys love to read about discoveries and adventures or to study numbers and proportions or to devour descriptions of strange animals and objects, while others confine their attention to machinery, from the simplest to the most complicated form. The point which these two types usually have in common is that the object in which they are interested must be a concrete one, not the product of fantasy like the fairy tales and fables enjoyed in early childhood, but something which has an actual physical existence. When the prepubertal period begins, a tendency for the concrete interests of the latency period to give place to abstractions becomes more and more marked. In particular, adolescents of the type which Bernfeld describes as characterized by "prolonged puberty" have an insatiable desire to think about abstract subjects, to turn them over in their minds, and to talk about them. Many of the friendships of youth are based on and maintained by this desire to meditate upon and discuss such subjects together. The range of these abstract interests and of the problems which these young people try to solve is very wide. They will argue the case for free love or marriage and family life, a free-lance existence or the adoption of a profession, roving or settling down, or discuss philosophical problems

such as religion or free thought, or different political theories, such as revolution versus submission to authority, or
friendship itself in all its forms. If, as sometimes happens
in analysis, we receive a faithful report of the conversations
of young people or if—as has been done by many of those
who make a study of puberty—we examine the diaries and
jottings of adolescents, we are not only amazed at the wide
and unfettered sweep of their thought but impressed by
the degree of empathy and understanding manifested, by
their apparent superiority to more mature thinkers, and
sometimes even by the wisdom which they display in their
handling of the most difficult problems.

We revise our opinion when we turn from the examination of the adolescent's intellectual processes themselves to
consider how they fit into the general picture of his life.
We are surprised to discover that this fine intellectual performance makes little or no difference to his actual behavior. His empathy into the mental processes of other
people does not prevent him from displaying the most
outrageous lack of consideration toward those nearest to
him. His lofty view of love and of the obligations of a lover
does not mitigate the infidelity and callousness of which
he is repeatedly guilty in his various love affairs. The fact
that his understanding of and interest in the structure of
society often far exceed those of later years does not assist
him in the least to find his true place in social life, nor does
the many-sidedness of his interests deter him from concentrating upon a single point—his preoccupation with his
own personality.

We recognize, especially when we come to investigate
these intellectual interests in analysis, that we have here
something quite different from intellectuality in the ordi-

nary sense of the term. We must not suppose that an adolescent ponders on the various situations in love or on the choice of a profession in order to think out the right line of behavior, as an adult might do or as a boy in the latency period studies a piece of machinery in order to be able to take it to pieces and put it together again. Adolescent intellectuality seems merely to minister to daydreams. Even the ambitious fantasies of the prepubertal period are not intended to be translated into reality. When a young lad fantasies that he is a great conqueror, he does not on that account feel any obligation to give proof of his courage or endurance in real life. Similarly, he evidently derives gratification from the mere process of thinking, speculating or discussing. His behavior is determined by other factors and is not necessarily influenced by the results of these intellectual gymnastics.

There is yet another point which strikes us when we analyze the intellectual processes of adolescents. A closer examination shows that the subjects in which they are principally interested are the very same as have given rise to the conflicts between the different psychic institutions. Once more, the point at issue is how to relate the instinctual side of human nature to the rest of life, how to decide between putting sexual impulses into practice and renouncing them, between liberty and restraint, between revolt against and submission to authority. As we have seen, asceticism, with its flat prohibition of instinct, does not generally accomplish what the adolescent hopes. Since the danger is omnipresent, he has to devise many means of surmounting it. The *thinking over* of the instinctual conflict— its intellectualization—would seem to be a suitable means. Here the ascetic flight from instinct is exchanged for a turning toward it. But this merely takes place in thought; it is an intellectual process. The abstract intellectual discussions and speculations in which young people delight are not genuine attempts at solving the tasks set by reality. Their mental activity is rather an indication of a tense alertness for the instinctual processes and the translation into abstract thought of that which they perceive. The philosophy of life which they construct—it may be their demand for revolution in the outside world—is really their response to the perception of the new instinctual demands of their own id, which threaten to revolutionize their whole lives. Their ideals of friendship and undying loyalty are simply a reflection of the disquietude of the ego when it perceives the evanescence of all its new and passionate object relations.[1] The longing for guidance and support in the often hopeless battle against their own powerful instincts may be transformed into ingenious arguments about man's inability to arrive at independent political decisions. We see then that instinctual processes are translated into terms of intellect. But the reason why attention is thus focused on the instincts is that an attempt is being made to lay hold of and master them on a different psychic level.

We remember that in psychoanalytic metapsychology the association of affects and instinctual processes with word representations is stated to be the first and most important step in the direction of the mastery of instinct which has to be taken as the individual develops. Thinking is described in these writings as "an experimental kind of acting, accompanied by displacement of relatively small quantities

---

[1] I am indebted to Margit Dubovitz, of Budapest, for the suggestion that the tendency of adolescents to brood on the meaning of life and death reflects the destructive activities in their own psyche.

of cathexis together with less expenditure (discharge) of them" (Freud, 1911, p. 221). This intellectualization of instinctual life, the attempt to lay hold on the instinctual processes by connecting them with ideas which can be dealt with in consciousness, is one of the most general, earliest, and most necessary acquirements of the human ego. We regard it not as an activity of the ego but as one of its indispensable components.

Once more we have the impression that the phenomena here comprised in the notion of "intellectualization at puberty" simply represent the exaggeration, under the peculiar conditions of a sudden accession of libido, of a general ego attitude. It is merely the increase in the quantity of libido which attracts attention to a function of the ego performed by it at other times as a matter of course, silently, and, as it were, by the way. If this is so, it means that the intensification of intellectuality during adolescence—and perhaps, too, the very marked advance in intellectual understanding of psychic processes which is always characteristic of an access of psychotic disease—is simply part of the ego's customary endeavor to master the instincts by means of thought.

Here, I think, we may note a secondary discovery to which this train of thought has led us. If it is true that an increase in libidinal cathexis invariably has the automatic effect of causing the ego to redouble its efforts to work over the instinctual processes intellectually, this would explain the fact that instinctual danger makes human beings intelligent. In periods of calm in the instinctual life, when there is no danger, the individual can permit himself a certain degree of stupidity. In this respect instinctual anxiety has the familiar effect of objective anxiety. Objective danger

and deprivations spur men on to intellectual feats and ingenious attempts to solve their difficulties, while objective
security and superfluity tend to make them comfortably
stupid. The focusing of the intellect on instinctual processes
is analogous to the alertness which the human ego has
found to be necessary in the face of the objective dangers
which surround it.

Hitherto the decline in the intelligence of little children
at the beginning of the latency period has been explained in
another way. In early childhood their brilliant intellectual
achievements are closely connected with their inquiries into
the mysteries of sex and, when this subject becomes taboo,
the prohibition and inhibition extend to other fields of
thought. No surprise has been felt at the fact that, with the
rekindling of sexuality in the prepubertal period, i.e., with
the breakdown of the sexual repression of early childhood,
the subject's intellectual capacities revive in all their old
strength.

This is the ordinary explanation, to which we may now
add a second. It may be that in the latency period children
not only *dare* not indulge in abstract thought: they may
have no need to do so. Infancy and puberty are periods of
instinctual danger and the "intelligence" which character-
izes them serves at least in part to assist the subject to sur-
mount that danger. In latency and adult life, on the other
hand, the ego is relatively strong and can without detriment
to the individual relax its efforts to intellectualize the instinctual processes. At the same time we must not forget
that these mental performances, especially at puberty, brilliant and remarkable as they are, remain to a great extent
unfruitful. This is true in one respect even of the intellectual feats of early childhood, which we admire and prize so

highly. We have only to think how the infantile sexual investigations, which psychoanalysis regards as the clearest manifestation of the child's intellectual activity, hardly ever lead to a knowledge of the true facts of adult sexual life. As a rule, they result in the construction of infantile sexual theories, which do not represent the reality but reflect the instinctual processes in the mind of the childish observer.

The intellectual work performed by the ego during the latency period and in adult life is incomparably more solid, more reliable, and, above all, much more closely connected with action.

OBJECT LOVE AND IDENTIFICATION AT PUBERTY

Let us now consider how the asceticism and intellectualization characteristic of puberty fit into our scheme of orientation of the defensive processes according to anxiety and danger. We see at once that both the methods in question come under the heading of the third type of defense. The danger which threatens the ego is that it may be submerged by the instincts; what it dreads above all is the *quantity* of instinct. We believe that this anxiety originates very early in the development of the individual. Chronologically, it belongs to the period during which an ego is gradually being isolated out of the undifferentiated id. The defensive measures which its dread of the strength of the instincts impels it to adopt are designed to maintain this differentiation between ego and id and to ensure the permanence of the newly established ego organization. The task which asceticism sets itself is to keep the id within limits by simply imposing prohibitions; the aim of intellectualization is to link up instinctual processes closely with ideational contents and so to render them accessible to consciousness and amenable to control.

Now when, with the sudden accession of libido, the individual falls back to this primitive level of dread of the strength of the instincts, the rest of the instinctual and ego processes are bound to be affected. In what follows I shall select two of the most important of the many peculiarities of puberty and trace their connéction with this process of ego regression.

The most remarkable phenomena in the life of adolescents are at bottom connected with their object relations. It is here that the conflict between two opposite tendencies is most visible. We have seen that the repression prompted by the general antagonism to instinct usually selects for its first attack the incestuous fantasies of the prepubertal period. The suspicion and asceticism of the ego are primarily directed against the subject's fixation to all the love objects of his childhood. The result of this is, on the one hand, that the young person tends to isolate himself; from this time on, he will live with the members of his family as though with strangers. But it is not only his relation to external love objects which attracts the ego's innate antagonism to instinct; his relation to the superego suffers likewise. Insofar as the superego is at this period still cathected with libido derived from the relation to the parents, it is itself treated as a suspicious incestuous object and falls a victim to the consequences of asceticism. The ego alienates itself from the superego as well. To young people this partial repression of the superego, the estrangement from part of its contents, is one of the greatest troubles of adolescence. The principal effect of the rupture of the relation between ego and superego is to increase the danger which threatens from the instincts. The individual tends to become asocial. Before this disturbance took place, the anxiety of conscience and sense of guilt which arose out of the relation of the ego to the superego were the former's most powerful allies in its struggle with the instincts. At the beginning of puberty there is often evidence of a transient attempt to effect a hypercathexis of all the contents of the superego. This is probably the explanation of the so-called "idealism" of adolescence. We now have the following situation: asceticism, itself due to an increase in instinctual danger, actually leads to the rupture of the relation with the superego and so renders inoperative the defensive measures prompted by superego anxiety, with the result that the ego is still more violently thrown back to the level of pure instinctual anxiety and the primitive protective mechanisms characteristic of that level.

Self-isolation and a turning away from love objects are not, however, the only tendencies which come into play in the object relations of adolescents. Many new attachments take the place of the repressed fixations to the love objects of childhood. Sometimes the individual becomes attached to young people of his own age, in which case the relation takes the form of passionate friendship or of actually being in love; sometimes the attachment is to an older person, whom he takes as his leader and who is clearly a substitute for the abandoned parent objects. While they last, these love relations are passionate and exclusive, but they are of short duration. Persons are selected as objects and abandoned without any consideration for their feelings, and others are chosen in their place. The abandoned objects are quickly and completely forgotten, but the form of the relation to them is preserved down to the minutest detail and is generally reproduced, with an exactness which almost suggests obsession, in the relation to the new object.

Besides this striking faithfulness to the love object we

note another peculiarity of the object relations at puberty. The adolescent does not aim so much at possessing himself of the object in the ordinary physical sense of the term as at assimilating himself as much as possible to the person who at the moment occupies the central place in his affection.

The changeableness of young people is a commonplace. In their handwriting, mode of speech, way of doing their hair, their dress, and all sorts of habits they are far more adaptable than at any other period of life. Often a single glance at an adolescent will tell us who is the older friend whom he admires. But their capacity for change goes even further. Their philosophy of life, their religion and politics alter, as they exchange one model for another, and, however often they change, they are always just as firmly and passionately convinced of the rightness of the views which they have so eagerly adopted. In this respect they resemble a type of patient, described by Helene Deutsch (1934), in a clinical work on the psychology of adults, as being on the borderline between neurosis and psychosis. She calls them persons of the "as if" type, because in every new object relation they live *as if* they were really living their own life and expressing their own feelings, opinions, and views.

In a young girl whom I analyzed the mechanism on which these processes of transformation are based was especially clear. Several times in the course of a single year she changed in this way from one friendship to another, from girls to boys and from boys to older women. On each occasion she did not merely become indifferent to the abandoned love object but conceived for the person in question a peculiar and violent dislike—verging on contempt—and felt that any accidental or unavoidable meeting be-

tween them was almost unbearable. After a good deal of
analytic work we finally discovered that these feelings toward her former friends were not her own at all. Every
time she changed her love object, she felt obliged to model
her behavior on and adopt the views of her new friend in all
sorts of matters relating to both her inner and her outward
life. So she no longer experienced her own affects but those
of the friend of the moment. Her dislike of the people she
had formerly loved was not really her own. By a process of
empathy she had come to share the feelings of her new
friend. Thus she was giving expression to the jealousy which
she fantasied that *he* felt toward everyone whom she had
once loved or to *his* (not her own) contempt for possible
rivals.

The psychic situation in this and similar phases of puberty may be described very simply. These passionate and
evanescent love fixations are not object relations at all, in
the sense in which we use the term in speaking of adults.
They are identifications of the most primitive kind, such as
we meet with in our study of early infantile development,
before any object love exists. Thus the fickleness characteristic of puberty does not indicate any inner change in the
love or convictions of the individual but rather a loss of
personality in consequence of a change in identification.

The processes revealed by the analysis of a fifteen-year-
old girl may perhaps throw some light on the part played
by this propensity for identification. My patient was an
exceptionally pretty and charming girl and already played
a part in her social circle, but in spite of this she was tormented with a frantic jealousy of a sister who was still only
a child. At puberty the patient gave up all her former interests and was thenceforth actuated by a single desire—to win

the admiration and love of the boys and men who were her friends. She fell violently in love, at a distance, with a boy rather older than herself, whom she used sometimes to meet at parties and dances. At this time she wrote me a letter, in which she expressed her doubts and worries in connection with this love affair.

"Please tell me," she wrote, "how to behave when I meet him. Ought I to be serious or gay? Will he like me better if I show that I am intelligent or if I pretend to be stupid? Would you advise me to talk about *him* the whole time, or shall I talk about myself too? . . ." When the patient next came to see me, I answered her questions verbally. I suggested that perhaps it was really not necessary to plan her behavior in advance. When the time came, could she not just be herself and behave as she felt? She assured me that that would never do and gave me a long dissertation on the necessity of suiting yourself to other people's preferences and wishes. She said that only in that way could you be sure of making them love you and, unless this boy loved her, she simply could not go on living.

Shortly afterward, this patient related a fantasy in which she pictured something like the end of the world. What would happen, she asked, if everybody died? She went through all her friends and relations, until finally she imagined herself left quite alone on the earth. Her voice, her emphasis, and the way in which she described all the details showed that this fantasy was a wish fulfillment. She enjoyed relating it and it caused her no anxiety.

At this point I reminded her of her passionate desire to be loved. The mere idea of one of her friends not liking her and of losing his love had sufficed, only the day before, to plunge her into despair. But who was to love her if she were the sole survivor of the human race? She calmly dismissed my reminder of her worries of the previous day. "In that case I should love myself," she said, as if at last she were rid of all her anxieties, and she heaved a deep sigh of relief.

This little analytic observation in the case of a particular patient does, I think, indicate something which is characteristic of certain object relations at puberty. The rupture of former relations, antagonism to the instincts, and asceticism all have the effect of delibidinizing the external world. The adolescent is in danger of withdrawing his object libido from those around him and concentrating it upon himself; just as he has regressed within the ego, so he may regress in his libidinal life from object love to narcissism. He escapes this danger by convulsive efforts to make contact once more with external objects, even if it can only be by way of his narcissism, that is, through a series of identifications. According to this view, the passionate object relations of adolescence represent attempts at recovery—another respect in which they resemble the state of psychotic patients whose disease is about to take one of its periodic turns for the worse.

In my account of puberty I have so often compared the peculiar characteristics of that period with the phenomena of grave disease that (although this study makes no pretense at completeness) I ought perhaps to say a word about the normality or abnormality of the processes which take place during this phase.

We have seen that the basis of comparison between puberty and the beginning of one of the periodic advances in psychotic disease is the effect which we attribute to quantitative changes in cathexis. In each case the heightened libidinal cathexis of the id adds to the instinctual danger, causing the ego to redouble its efforts to defend itself in every possible way. It has always been realized in psychoanalysis that, because of these quantitative processes, every period in human life during which libido is increased may be the starting point of neurotic or psychotic disease.

Secondarily, puberty and such accesses of psychosis resemble one another in the emergence of primitive defensive attitudes which we associate with the ego's dread of the strength of the instincts—an anxiety which goes further back than any objective anxiety or anxiety of conscience.

The impression which we receive of the normality or abnormality of the processes at puberty in any individual will probably depend upon whether there is a predominance of one or other of the characteristics which I have enumerated or of several of them at once. The ascetic adolescent strikes us as normal, so long as his intellect functions freely and he has a number of healthy object relations. A similar proviso applies to adolescents of the type which intellectualizes instinctual processes, to those of the idealistic type, and also to those who are carried headlong from one enthusiastic friendship to another. But, if the ascetic attitude is rigorously maintained, if the process of intellectualization overruns the whole field of mental life, and if relations to other people are based exclusively on changing identincations, it will be difficult for a teacher or analyst to decide from observation how much may still be regarded as a transitional phase in normal development and how much is already pathological.

Conclusion

In the foregoing chapters I have tried to classify the various defense mechanisms according to the specific anxiety situations which call them into action and I have illustrated my remarks by a number of clinical examples. As our knowledge of the unconscious activity of the ego advances, a much more precise classification will probably become possible. There is still considerable obscurity about the historical connection between typical experiences in individual development and the production of particular modes of defense. My examples suggest that the typical situations in which the ego has recourse to the mechanism of denial are those associated with ideas of castration and with the loss of love objects. On the other hand, the altruistic surrender of instinctual impulses seems, under certain conditions, to be a specific means of overcoming narcissistic mortification.

In the present state of our knowledge we can already speak with greater certainty about the parallels between the ego's defensive measures against external and against internal danger. *Repression* gets rid of instinctual derivatives, just as external stimuli are abolished by *denial. Reaction formation* secures the ego against the return of repressed impulses from within, while by *fantasies in which the real situation is reversed* denial is sustained against overthrow from without. *Inhibition* of instinctual impulses corresponds to the *restrictions* imposed on the ego to avoid unpleasure from external sources. *Intellectualization* of the instinctual processes as a precaution against danger from within is analogous to the constant *alertness* of the ego to dangers from without. All the other defensive measures which, like reversal and turning against the subject, entail an alteration in the instinctual processes themselves have their counterpart in the ego's attempts to deal with the external danger by actively intervening to change the conditions of the world around it. Upon this last side of the ego's activities I cannot enlarge here.

This comparison of parallel processes suggests the question: whence does the ego derive the form of its defense mechanisms? Is the struggle with the outside forces modeled on the conflict with the instincts? Or is the converse the case: are the measures adopted in the external struggle the prototype of the various defense mechanisms? The decision between these two alternatives can hardly be a straightforward one. The infantile ego experiences the onslaught of instinctual and external stimuli at the same time; if it wishes to preserve its existence it must defend itself on both sides simultaneously. In the struggle with the different kinds of stimuli which it has to master it probably adapts its weapons to the particular need, arming itself now against danger from within and now against danger from without.

How far does the ego follow its own laws in its defense against the instincts and how far is it influenced by the character of the instincts themselves? Perhaps some light may be thrown on this problem by a comparison with an analogous process, that of *dream distortion*. The translation of latent dream thoughts into the manifest dream content is carried out at the behest of the censor, i.e., the representative of the ego in sleep. But the dream work itself is not performed by the ego. Condensation, displacement, and the many strange modes of representation which occur in dreams are processes peculiar to the id and are merely utilized for the purpose of distortion. In the same way the various measures of defense are not entirely the work of the ego. Insofar as the instinctual processes themselves are modified, use is made of the peculiar properties of instinct. For instance, the readiness with which such processes can be *displaced* assists the mechanism of *sublimation*, by which the ego achieves its purpose of diverting the instinctual impulses from their purely sexual goal to aims which society holds to be higher. Again, in securing repressions by means of *reaction formation* the ego avails itself of the instinct's capacity for *reversal*. We may conjecture that a defense is proof against attack only if it is built up on this twofold basis—on the one hand, the ego and, on the other, the essential nature of instinctual processes.

But, even when we admit that the ego has not an entirely free hand in devising the defense mechanisms which it employs, our study of these mechanisms impresses us with the magnitude of its achievement. The existence of neurotic symptoms in itself indicates that the ego has been overpowered, and every return of repressed impulses, with its sequel in compromise formation, shows that some plan for defense has miscarried and the ego has suffered a defeat. But the ego is victorious when its defensive measures effect their purpose, i.e., when they enable it to restrict the development of anxiety and unpleasure and so to transform the instincts that, even in difficult circumstances, some measure of gratification is secured, thereby establishing the most harmonious relations possible between the id, the superego, and the forces of the outside world.

Bibliography

ALEXANDER, F. (1933), The Relation of Structural and Instinctual Conflicts. *Psychoanal. Quart.*, 2:181-207.

ANGEL, A. (1934), Einige Bemerkungen über den Optimismus. *Int. Z. Psychoanal.*, 20:191-199.

BERNFELD, S. (1923), Über eine typische Form der männlichen Pubertät. *Imago*, 9:169-188.

BORNSTEIN, B. (1936), Ein Beispiel für die Leugnung durch die Phantasie. *Z. psychoanal. Päd.*, 10:269-275.

BREUER, J. & FREUD, S. (1893-1895), Studies on Hysteria. *Standard Edition*, 2.*

DEUTSCH, H. (1933), The Psychology of Manic-Depressive States, with Particular Reference to Chronic Hypomania. In: *Neuroses and Character Types: Clinical Psychoanalytic Studies.* New York: International Universities Press, 1965, pp. 203-217.

——— (1934), Some Forms of Emotional Disturbances and Their Relationship to Schizophrenia. In: *Neuroses and Character Types: Clinical Psychoanalytic Studies.* New York: International Universities Press, 1965, pp. 262-281.

* See footnote †.

FEDERN, P. (1936), On the Distinction between Healthy and Pathological Narcissism. In: *Ego Psychology and the Psychoses*. London: Hogarth Press, 1952, pp. 323-364.

FREUD, ANNA (1926-1927), Introduction to the Technique of Child Analysis. In: *The Psycho-Analytical Treatment of Children*. London: Hogarth Press, 1955.

FREUD, SIGMUND (1894), The Neuro-Psychoses of Defence. *Standard Edition*, 3:45-61.†

——— (1896a), Further Remarks. on the Neuro-Psychoses of Defence. *Standard Edition*, 3:162-185.

——— (1896b), The Aetiology of Hysteria. *Standard Edition*, 3:191-221.

——— (1905), Three Essays on the Theory of Sexuality. *Standard Edition*, 7:125-245.

——— (1909), Analysis of a Phobia in a Five-Year-Old Boy. *Standard Edition*, 10:5-149.

——— (1911), Formulations on the Two Principles of Mental Functioning. *Standard Edition*, 12:215-226.

——— (1913), Totem and Taboo. *Standard Edition*, 13:1-161.

——— (1915), Instincts and Their Vicissitudes. *Standard Edition*, 14:109-140.

——— (1920), Beyond the Pleasure Principle. *Standard Edition*, 18:3-64.

——— (1921), Group Psychology and the Analysis of the Ego. *Standard Edition*, 18:67-147.

——— (1922), Some Neurotic Mechanisms in Jealousy, Paranoia and Homosexuality. *Standard Edition*, 18:221-232.

——— (1923), The Ego and the Id. *Standard Edition*, 19:3-66.

——— (1926), Inhibitions, Symptoms and Anxiety. *Standard Edition*, 20:77-175.

——— (1933), New Introductory Lectures on Psycho-Analysis. *Standard Edition*, 22:3-182.

HALL, J. WAELDER (1946), The Analysis of a Case of Night Ter-

† *The Standard Edition of the Complete Psychological Works of Sigmund Freud*, 24 Volumes, translated and edited by James Strachey. London: Hogarth Press and the Institute of Psycho-Analysis, 1953-

ror. *The Psychoanalytic Study of the Child*, 2:189-228. London: Hogarth Press.

JONES, E. (1922), Some Problems of Adolescence. *Papers on Psycho-Analysis*. London: Baillière, Tindall & Cox, 5th ed., 1948, pp. 389-406.

KATAN, A., *see* Angel, A.

KLEIN, M. (1932), *The Psychoanalysis of Children*. London: Hogarth Press, 1960.

LAFORGUE, R. (1928), Überlegungen zum Begriff der Verdrängung. *Int. Z. Psychoanal.*, 14:371-374.

LEWIN, B. D. (1932), Analysis and Structure of a Transient Hypomania. *Psychoanal. Quart.*, 1:43-58.

RÁDO, S. (1933), Fear of Castration in Women. *Psychoanal. Quart.*, 2:425-475.

RANK, O. (1909), *The Myth of the Birth of the Hero*. New York: Nervous and Mental Diseases Publishing Co., 1914.

REICH, W. (1933), *Charakteranalyse: Technik und Grundlagen für studierende und praktizierende Analytiker*. Vienna: Selbstverlag. [English: *Character-Analysis*. New York: Noonday Press, 1949.]

WAELDER, J., *see* Hall, J. Waelder.

WAELDER, R. (1930), The Principle of Multiple Function. *Psychoanal. Quart.*, 5:45-62, 1936.

Index